HOW TO BAG
THE BIGGEST BUCK
OF YOUR LIFE

HOW TO BAG
THE BIGGEST BUCK
OF YOUR LIFE

LARRY BENOIT
AND
PETER MILLER

Illustrations by
Ed Vebell

Photographs by
Peter Miller and John Randolph

THE LYON'S PRESS
Guilford, Connecticut
An imprint of The Globe Pequot Press

The Lyons Press is an imprint of The Globe Pequot Press.

10 9 8 7 6 5 4 3 2 1

Printed in the United States of America

Designed by Peter Holm, Sterling Hill Productions

ISBN 1-59228-099-4

Library of Congress Cataloging-in-Publication data is available on file.

In loving memory of my father, Uncle Shine, and my oldest brother Carl. Dad and Uncle Shine instilled in me the joy and thrill of hunting. In the few years that Carl and I hunted together we became more than brothers and close hunting companions. He was my hero.

Contents

Introduction

Alone far in the wilds and mountains I hunt,
Wandering amazed at my own lightness and glee...
—Walt Whitman, *Song Of Myself*

Although Larry Benoit was a whitetail hunter of legendary prowess back in the spring of 1970, not very many people knew about him at that time. The remote Vermont mountains where he stalked and tracked bucks of mind-boggling size were the setting of a drama yet to open to the public. The curtain would go up in September, set in motion by a series of events in New York the previous spring. I know exactly what happened. I was there.

It all started over a lunch, an old-fashioned publishing lunch.

Today the two-fisted, no-holds-barred luncheons that were once part of the magazine publishing game—book publishing as well—are gone. Were Ernest Hemingway shown to a table in one of the Manhattan bistros favored by publishing honchos today, he would be shocked at what he saw on the tables. No martinis, daiquiris, or amber glasses of whiskey. In their stead would lurk designer bottles of spring water, outriders to plates with smears of spinach-looking green salads and vegetables and pieces of baked chicken (skin removed, thank you) about the circumference and thickness of a 50-cent piece. Nouvelle cuisine. *Poulet Tasteless.* $34.50 *prix fixe.*

For better or for worse, things weren't always this way.

In the spring of 1970 in New York, nouvelle cuisine and healthy eating habits had not yet become the luncheon of choice for writers, agents, editors, or advertising executives armed with expense accounts. In the

Black Angus Restaurant on Lexington Avenue, just down the street from the *Sports Afield* magazine offices where I had been given the editorial reins in March, Peter Miller and I were knocking back some wonderful wine and a couple of slabs of prime rib we figured had once been part of a real Black Angus. At that time, Peter had become a contributor whose work I had been immensely pleased to get into the pages of the magazine. He was a freelancer then, from Vermont, but was a veteran of New York magazine corridors with such esteemed "books"—as magazine insiders call other magazines—as *Life* and *Sports Illustrated*. As experienced as a writer and editor Peter was at that time, his talent as a photographer was awesome. His images were fresh and exciting and vivid with light and shadows and angles that captured the true outdoors with both force and subtleness.

Discovering Peter and his work had been nothing short of a coup for me on behalf of the readers of *Sports Afield*. At that time the circulation numbered almost 1.5 million. "That's a lot of folks," I used to tell both our contributors and our advertising people and their clients, recalling a little fantasy image of mine.

As editor of *Sports Afield* in that spring of 1970, I was feeling a great sense of pride (at 33, it was my good fortune to be the youngest editor of a major national magazine at that time) tempered by the pressing need to revitalize the magazine. I had worked under the tutelage of Ted Kesting since joining the magazine as an associate editor in 1967 and was honored to succeed him. His great run as editor of *Sports Afield* had begun in the 1940s while the magazine was still in Minneapolis. When Hearst purchased *Sports Afield* in 1953, the company literally "purchased" Ted Kesting with it, and since then he had brought the magazine into the modern era.

Now he would continue to give me his advice and counsel, but I would have to call the plays. And, as they say in football, I had better "make some plays."

The situation I found myself in was, and still is, fairly typical in the magazine business. Any new editor's marching orders include such phrases as "a fresh, new look"..."more reader reward"..."more upscale approach" ...blah...blah. The clichés are thrown around like loose change, which is just about what they are worth as advice. For no matter how loud the clamor for the new and fresh, the voices of caution are always there, admonishing editors, as in medicine, to "first do no harm." In my case, some of the phrases I was hearing were much more interesting, including: "Kid, don't maintain the status quo. On the other hand, don't throw the baby out with the bathwater." Meaning: We want new advertisers, new subscribers, and newsstand buyers. But don't lose the ones we already have.

Over our prime rib that spring day in 1970, while Peter Miller and I were discussing ways to improve *Sports Afield,* he came up with a startling suggestion. He was working on a piece on a Vermont deer hunter named Larry Benoit. Peter described him as an amazing tracker whose technique was to get on the trail of a buck and hunt it down over miles of mountain terrain. His sons were all deer hunters too, and together they had become legends in the remote region where they lived, near Duxbury. "When you read the piece I'm writing," Peter said, "you're going to see that Larry Benoit may be the best deer hunter in America. And whether he is or not, he's certainly the most interesting. Why not put him on the cover?"

There it was: The big idea I had been searching for in ramping up a newer, fresher *Sports Afield.* But was it too radical? That kind of cover was from the realms of books like *Sports Illustrated.* No outdoor magazine had ever run a journalistic cover like Peter was suggesting. Mostly the covers had always been paintings of dramatic hunting and fishing scenes, the buck running, the fish jumping. A photograph of a man we're calling the best deer hunter in America? Readers might hate it—and hate us for running it instead of a traditional painting. I could see my fledgling career as editor coming to an abrupt end. Across town, our competitors— Clare Conley of *Field & Stream* and Chet Fish of *Outdoor Life*—would be laughing. Bill Rae and Hugh Grey, the great *Outdoor Life* and *Field & Stream* editors of the past, would be shaking their heads.

Nevertheless, my gut told me that Peter was right. Provided Peter would come through with a story and photos as powerful as he was describing, the Larry Benoit cover could be the signature event to launch a better *Sports Afield*.

I don't think I've ever begun reading a manuscript with more anticipation than I did when Peter's story and transparencies arrived on my desk a couple of weeks later. The very first paragraph left me thunderstruck. It began: "They live, breed and die on the mountaintops — far removed from the valleys, which are pierced by roads and blotted by houses, shops, gas fumes, man noise and man smell." I continued on, caught up in the irresistible prose of one of the finest deer stories I have ever read. The photographs were just as strong: vivid images of Larry Benoit and his sons.

Although I felt absolutely positive that the Benoit cover was a go, I consulted eagerly with Ted Kesting and some of our other editors, and even showed the cover to Hearst management. There was never a negative view, nor a pause. As far as everyone was concerned we could not get the cover in print fast enough.

In the final week of August, 1970, the September

issue of *Sports Afield* began going on sale throughout the United States and Canada with the Larry Benoit face on the cover, sighting down the barrel of his Remington pump .30-06, and a blurb which read: "Larry Benoit—Is He the Best Deer Hunter In America?" Inside the magazine, which was a showcase of new graphics, Peter Miller's story about Larry was titled "Ridge Runner Whitetails: They Take a Special Breed of Deer Hunter" and was presented on three color and two black-and-white pages. The magazine cost 50 cents. Today, I have been told, collectors will pay $500 for one of those September copies. I don't know who or where these collectors are, however.

The magazine was on the stands. Life went on. Planning other issues, moving ahead, I lived in a state of constant suspense over what would happen. I had convinced myself that this was going to result in either a great triumph or great disaster. In my view, nothing in between was possible.

I was wrong. The month passed. The October issue went onto the stands. The Larry Benoit issue was gone.

Finally, the sales figures began to come in. I winced when I saw the sheet of numbers in my in-box. I picked it up.

Nothing had happened. There was no disaster, there was no great triumph. The magazine sold the same number of copies it always sold in September. No big deal.

I was still puzzling over this some weeks later when I began to hear things about that September issue. My friend John Marsman of Savage told me that in his entire career he had never heard so much comment about a single issue of any outdoor magazine. Favorable comment, to boot.

As things have turned out, John Marsman's remark was the beginning of the fulfillment of all my fervent wishes for the success of the Larry Benoit presentation. I began to pick up other comments. I had no medals to show, if you will, but I felt that the campaign had been a success. So much so that I eventually asked for four more Larry Benoit pieces for our *Sports Afield* readers. When they ran, with superb illustrations by artist Ed Vebell, their presence in *Sports Afield* set the next phase of the Larry Benoit legend in motion when Larry and Peter Miller arranged for all the material to be collected and supplemented in a book called "How to Bag the Biggest Buck of Your Life," by Larry Benoit with Peter Miller.

Since first being printed in January, 1975, "How to Bag the Biggest Buck of Your Life" has quite literally become a legendary book. Used copies are commonly priced at over $400 on internet sites like alibris.com, abebooks.com, and bibliofind.com. Now there is no denying that the whitetail deer is the greatest game animal in North America (heck, perhaps the world!). And there are a lot of good books on hunting the whitetail. Why has this one become a sort of publishing legend? Larry Benoit is not a showman. He has not traveled the nation, promoting his book in the media, appearing on network television shows. How then have Larry and his sons become figures of almost cult status, with a following of deeply interested sportsmen?

My personal opinion on the subject is not offered as an "expert witness," or even as an editor. It is as a reader, dedicated to enjoying hunting in print, if you will, that I share with you the feeling of what I find in the pages of "How to Bag the Biggest Buck of Your Life."

First, the prose is superb. From the first section on "Ridge Runner Bucks," which I mentioned earlier, to a final chapter on Larry's thoughts about what being a deer hunter means to him, the book reads beautifully. It is engaging and illuminating, the words flowing seamlessly, it seems to me, through personal experiences and observations into practical hardcore advice. There is action galore. Accounts of Larry's hunts and some of his sons' hunts carry the reader with them following the whitetail tracks into the rugged mountains. There is here what the distinguished English novelist E. M. Forster called "a felt life."

Beyond the "remember when" and "how-to" the book captures so splendidly, I sense a spirit of frontier-like freedom and opportunity. Larry Benoit looks at the mountains as our pioneer forefathers saw them. For the Larry Benoits of the world there are no boundaries, no posted signs, no stands where you must sit to bag your buck. Sit because you have nowhere else to go. Let's face it: There a lot of whitetail deer out there, but not many of us can hunt them where we are free to follow a trail wherever it leads us. Those who can are indeed fortunate. The average Joe, however, must stick to the small plot where he has permission to hunt. To stray means to be arrested for trespassing. Or worse, shot by a careless hunter. Hunting in the Larry Benoit style is admired and envied at the same time. As much as we enjoy reading about it, not many of us can emulate Larry's hunting style. In my case, even if I had hundreds of acres of wilderness to hunt over, I would likely have a heart attack trying to hunt like Larry. (In fact, in the book he warns about this very point.) I am not a young man, and a slower pace has to dictate my tactics now. Still, I like following Larry in print, sharing what I can from the comfort of an easy chair.

Another thing I think readers have appreciated about Larry Benoit and his hunting is that he is a family man, dedicated to raising his sons to share the hunting trails with him. The fact that Larry's sons are great hunters says a lot about his character and strengths. He obviously has taken the time and care to share with his boys what they need to know to be good hunters and good men.

This new and very welcome edition of "How to Bag the Biggest Buck of Your Life" will likely spread the "Larry Benoit Mystique," if that's what you want to call it, to new generations of readers and hunters. Like others before them, they will look at Larry and his sons and how they hunt, and they will say to themselves: "Yes. Those guys are good! I'd like to hunt that way myself."

I hope they get the chance.

In the meantime, my hunting cap is off to Larry and Peter and what they have accomplished in print. I am delighted I played a small part in bringing all this into being.

At Hearst, which owned *Sports Afield* during my years with the magazine, I had the great privilege of knowing Wade Nichols, the Editor of Hearst's flagship magazine, *Good Housekeeping.* Wade, who is gone now, once said to me: "Lamar, do you know what good editors do? It's not all the management stuff. It's not changing commas and whipping manuscripts into shape. What good editors do is this: They *find things.*"

They find things.

Well, I guess I qualify. I found Peter Miller. He found Larry Benoit. And we all brought something very special to the readers of *Sports Afield* and then the readers of this book. In the pages that lie ahead, you will see that the whitetail hunting experiences captured by Larry Benoit and Peter Miller's photographs are as vivid and alive as ever. Without doubt, Larry Benoit and his sons are a special breed of deer hunter. This is *their* book and *their* story.

Lamar Underwood
April, 2003

Acknowledgments

Many people—friends new and old—have urged me to write a book, and without their help and enthusiasm I just never would have gotten around to it. For years, Iris my wife has prodded me to write about my hunting experiences. Her enthusiasm for hunting and her love over the years are really what has made this book possible. Even before our babies came, she was my companion in the woods. She also has a lot of understanding and compassion to put up with me when the hunting season draws me, day after day, to the ridges.

My children have also whetted my love for hunting and teaching. It was a joy to take them with me, as they grew old enough, and to show them the lore of the woods and the track of the buck. I took my first born, Lanny, into the woods at the age of four to learn the art of tracking and the love of the woods. One by one, as the other boys grew older, I took them with me—Lance, Lane, and Shane. All of them are the best hunters and tracker I know, and I for one don't think any hunter in Vermont could do as well as Lanny does locating the trophy buck.

My daughters also learned to hunt when they were young, but they have found more happiness in love and marriage and little ones. They also put up with their dad every deer season rising at dawn and returning late at night.

I also wish to acknowledge the help of Uncle Windy Lawrence. When the first snow hits the brow of the highest mountain, Uncle Windy is not far behind. He has accompanied me on hunts for the past 40 years. The old goat is a great story teller and out of his love for me and my sons he gave the final push for me to publish this book.

Peter Miller is a fellow Vermonter who lives just down the road from me. He calls himself the worst deer hunter in Vermont but the best of woodcock hunters. He is a photographer and writer and it was through his curiosity and journalism that I started to write articles. He helped put this book in shape, sweating over it in his garret office and not getting out enough to hunt woodcock. He's a good writer and photographer, but a better friend.

I also wish to thank Lamar Underwood, editor of *Sports Afield.* He has published four of my articles and it was the letters I received from hunters all over the United States that encouraged me to put down in this book what I have learned about trophy buck hunting over the past 40 years.

L.E.B.

Foreword

For well over half a century I have known the Benoits. I have hunted with Larry Benoit's grandfather, his father Leo, and for years I have shared hunting experiences with Ling (the family name for Larry) and his son, Lanny. That's more years than I care to think about, but they were rich years. Ling's father Leo was a remarkable man. He was strong enough to wrestle an ox to the floor, if that ox cared to give him any trouble when Leo was shoeing him. He was also an uncanny woodsman and tracker and he brought up his sons in the tradition of tracking and bagging the biggest buck they could find in northern Vermont. Larry was just a little whippersnapper when Leo taught him to hunt. The first time Leo let Ling use a rifle, he gave him three shells and told him to shoot three squirrels. The little runt took the three .22 cartridges and came back with three squirrels. That was the first time that Leo knew that Larry was out hunting with a rifle. Later Leo would take Ling into the woods and point out a nice buck track and let Ling unravel it.

Ling was a headstrong shaver and one thing he lived for more than anything else was hunting. He listened carefully to his father and he learned quickly. He taught himself how to shoot. Ling, using a .22 or the old 25/20, helped supply meat during the Depression. He brought home not only squirrels but woodchucks, hedgehogs, and partridges. He rarely wasted shells.

Ling shot his first buck when he as nine. Leo gave him the 45/70 with two cartridges and told Ling not to miss. That little fellow trudged up the side of a big mountain, trailed a trophy buck, and nailed him with one shot. Ling was small for his age, weighed around 60 pounds and the 45/70 would kick hell out of him. That buck was so big that Ling couldn't even roll him over. He cut off the buck's testicles and took them home to show his father and me. We all grabbed jugs of hard cider and hitched the horse on a pung and promptly marched back into the woods, backtracking Ling's path until we found the buck. By 2:00 in the morning, the cider was gone and we still hadn't reached the buck, he was so high on the mountain. We finally located the buck, built a huge fire to warm ourselves, and finished dressing out the deer. We were back home by dawn. I remember that even then some of the men were jealous of young Ling.

Another time Leo wouldn't allow Ling to hunt with us, and Ling, mad as all get out, took the 25/20 and hitched the horse to a sleigh, threw a couple of deer skin robes over him, loaded a bundle of hay and took right off on a logging road. On the way he passed us with our car stuck in a ditch. Ling paid no attention and drove past into a basin, bagged a nice six-pointer, cleaned him out, and dragged him right off the side of the mountain. He was too small to load the buck onto the sleigh so he tied it to the back by the antlers and headed for home, lickety-split. His father and I were still stuck but all Ling did when he drove by was to yell at us, "If you don't let me go hunting with you, then pull your own car out!" That year Ling was the only one to bag a deer, and his father never again kept him from hunting.

Ling is a born hunter, and I knew he'd be a great nimrod when he took me out one afternoon when he couldn't have been more than eight. We came upon some deer tracks and Ling said to me, "See that?"

"Looks like turkey scratchings to me," I said.

"No, that's a buck track. He's pawing just like the bull does in the pasture."

A little further on the kid showed me where a buck was rubbing and I knew that little cuss would be some hell of a hunter. He was already good at tracking squirrels, rabbits, and foxes.

We followed the track and then Ling said it was a nice buck. Now I'm beginning to listen.

"How do you know?" I asked.

"Well," he said, "see how his tracks go out? Big deer do that, not little ones, and I'll also tell you how many points he has—six to eight."

"Go on!" I said. Then he took me back where the buck had been feeding and pointed to small holes in the snow.

"See the marks in the snow? That's where the antlers hit. Count 'em."

At that early age he was teaching me how to use my eyes. Ling always felt the challenge of going after the biggest buck, and he felt the challenge lay high in the mountains. Coming from mountain stock, a blend of French Canadian and Iroquois, I guess he just couldn't help it.

After Ling married and began raising a family, he passed on what he knew to his sons. He taught them the love of the woods and the lore of the deer. When Ling's eldest son, Lanny, was seven, Ling had him staying in the back woods by himself so he would never fear the wilderness. Ling taught Lanny some of the tracker's lore, but Lanny, as his father had done, figured out much of it himself, for being a good tracker is a gift. You can be told the fundamentals, but you have to go out and do it.

When Lanny was 16 he thought he was a pretty good

tracker. One time we were walking up a log road and Lanny was checking out a track but wasn't sure if it was a buck. His grandfather came along, gave a quick glance at the track and said to Lanny, "There's a helluva nice buck track right there. Why don't you take that one?" Lanny couldn't believe it, but within 100 yards he found where the buck scraped his antlers. Now I would say Lanny is a match for his father and will carry on that Benoit hunting instinct and pass it on to his children.

Many people just don't believe the success of the Benoit family. (Ling and Lanny happen to be the best right now. But the whole family has hunted, and hunted well, and that includes daughters and sons.) Lots of hunters have become jealous of their success. When we brought two huge bucks back from Maine before Vermont deer season opened, the local game warden received about 15 anonymous calls, all saying the Benoits has two illegal deer strung up on their porch.

Most hunters that we meet outside the Benoit home, where their deer are hung, are just amazed. They can't believe it. They listen and ask innumerable questions about how he bags such big bucks. It's hard for Ling to explain because so much of his deer tracking lore comes natural to him.

For years I have told him he should put it in a book. Well, he finally has, and I hope you learn as much from it as Ling has taught me, for in this book are the honest facts distilled from a life of a hunter who enjoys the chase much more than the killing. And that's what real hunting is all about. Listen carefully to this hunter. You won't go wrong.

Uncle Windy Lawrence

Preface

This is a simple, plain talking common sense and no nonsense book on hunting the Whitetail. I think the Whitetail is the greatest game animal in the world. It is the smartest, wildest, most curious, most beautiful, and wonderful and majestic animal in the woods. There are not enough words in the English language to describe the Whitetail. It has my utmost respect. The true nature of this animal can never be written down in one book.

There have been many stories, articles, and books written on the Whitetail, but none that I have read really get into the true facts about hunting the Whitetail. Since childhood I have studied these deer. I have practically lived with them. For over 40 years I have watched them play and feed and even make love. I have analyzed their tracks, their range, their hidden signs, their feeding patterns. I have seen them when they have been frightened, angry, and even belligerent. I have learned to feel in my gut the excitement of a big trophy buck out there in front of me, matching his acute senses against my wits. I have gotten to know the trophy bucks as they have left a trail in front of me from the Canadian border to the Coast of Maine and back to the Berkshires.

This, then, is my book about what I have learned during years of tracking and hunting and bagging trophy bucks. The ideas in this book were not borrowed from some other hunter, nor were they borrowed from the pages of some other book or some sports writers. They are my ideas on how to hunt the wiliest game animal I will ever meet. You may not agree with these principles, but that is not for me to argue. I know my methods are successful. The meat is on the table every year, and it is usually from one very big trophy buck.

As such, this book describes my methods. I am a tracker, as was my dad, and my Indian forebears. I hunt in the traditional, early American way. I go where no other hunter usually dares to go—deep in the woods and high on the ridges. I search for only the biggest bucks I can find, and I track only the biggest track that I run across. Sometimes a hunt for a trophy buck lasts only a few days, other times it can last for two weeks. But I believe once you find a track, you ought to read that track and be able to meet up with what you're tracking and bag an old hoosier.

Now I have shot the granddaddy of bucks. I have shot the brothers and the cousins and the sons and the uncles. But mister, I have yet to bag the biggest buck of my life. I'm still searching. And I hope that this book will help you on the quest for the biggest buck of your life.

Larry Benoit
Duxbury, Vermont

This book is dedicated
to all Whitetail deer hunters.

HOW TO BAG
THE BIGGEST BUCK
OF YOUR LIFE

−1−
THE TROPHY BUCK

They live, breed, and die on the mountain tops, far removed from valleys pierced by roads and blotted by houses, shops, gas fumes, man noise, and man scent. They course those small mountain streams that are pure as freshly fallen snow. They browse on moss by hidden springs that are fountainheads for lakes, and they feed on beechnuts, leaves, and buds. They bed down on small hillocks, where the trees are often stunted by the altitude. In winter, when the hoarfrost whitens the mountaintops and the winds is sharp, they browse their way down the mountain to the basin swamps, their winter habitat. In spring as the sun rises high over the vernal equinox, they follow the buds that redden the mountainsides. The sharp wind turn sweet, refreshing, and blow the flies away from their nose and eyes and rack. Their mark is an awful big track. They are the ridge runners, the prize studs of the American deer herd. In four years they grow to over 200 pounds and have thick, knobby racks. What appears to be moss on the base of their racks is actually flakes of bark from saplings that the buck has scraped as he polishes his rack and lessens the itch that antlers cause in his scalp. These mossy horns, as they are called, live long lives and are rarely seen, rarely shot.

The counterparts to the ridge runners are the swamp

bucks that also grow to a huge heft and are rarely disturbed. They hide in swamps and are often heard tearing through the thickets when disturbed. Heard, but rarely seen.

These are the Whitetail trophy bucks. They are different from the lowland or pasture bucks that mix with cow herds and feed in mowings and on apple trees and are used to human noise. The true old ridge runner, the buck I like to hunt for, is not all balled up with a lot of fat like the lowland buck. He is bigger and older because he is not hunted as much. He has been in more scraps and has kicked the heck out of the young bucks and not many things worry this mountain buck. After he has been around six or seven years, he's not scared of much, not even the hunter. He just lopes off while the young deer are all skitterish.

During the rut season the big ridge runner's neck swells. He is not so much interested in feeding as he is roaming. That buck is looking for does. These big devils spoil for fights with other bucks, and when they're in the love mood, they will take care of as many does as they can find. Once, while tracking, I saw one huge buck catch one herd of does and make love to three of them. Then he came onto another herd, piled into a smaller buck and pounded the hell out of him and mounted the does. Through with them he swung towards the top of the mountain, still searching for does, when I caught up to him.

Some of these bucks are barrel-chested. Others are long legged and can reel off many miles per day at a trot. Some have long bodies, others are short and squatty. Along the Canadian border Whitetails are a little different from our ordinary Eastern deer. They have longer legs, longer necks, and their hair is slightly red-

A buck that got away. He would go about 255, and he had 10 points. A 30-06 cartridge lies in the track.

dish. My dad called them the old slant-eyed mountain ridge runners, or greyfaced bucks. They are as tough to get as any other mountain cruiser. All of them, regardless of their physical build, are trophy bucks.

You know, anybody can shoot a deer, but it takes a mighty good hunter to go out and shoot a ridge running trophy buck whose track is so big you can lay a 30-06 cartridge in it. I'm talking of a deer that, dressed out, hits the scales over 200 pounds and has 10 or 12 points. This is a trophy buck and the way I look at it, if I can't get a mossy horn, I don't want anything less. One season I passed up five bucks I could have shot any time I wanted, but they weren't any match in size and heft for the old hoosier that I was tracking. I have run across three bucks at once, while tracking a monster buck, and shooed them away. This is not boasting—it is the simple fact that if you want a trophy buck, you have to have the discipline to stay after him until you down him. It is thrilling to be able to trail a monster buck and get him in your sights, to know you have outwitted him. Many hunters say they just want to get a buck, period, and they don't care how big the horns are. They have the limp excuse of saying, "Well, you can't eat the antlers!" I think they are missing the point. Those people that shoot spikehorns and smaller deer, and even does in some states, are not proving to themselves they are hunters. They are settling for something less than they should.

To outwit the Whitetail you must know how to locate him, how to track him, and how to down him. It takes stamina, woods lore, deer lore, and experience to win this fight. It takes a dedication of the will, the mind, the senses, and the body. You must put 100% of everything you have into the hunt for the trophy buck, or you won't win. This is one of the reasons I love to hunt the Whitetail—it requires all the experience and the skill and concentration and strength I have. It is the spirit of hunting, the challenge, and it is a mighty big challenge. It is the thrill of the hunt and, friend, when you are on a trophy buck, and you feel that perhaps the biggest buck of your life is only about 100 yards in front of you, and you have to move in on him, then you know what hunting is about. You will have this experience if you go on the quest, deep in the woods and mountains, and scout out that trophy buck.

−2−
CONDITIONING

At the end of the winter, particularly if it has been a hard one, the deer are weak, sometimes even near starvation. They have yarded up, usually browsing on hemlock and spruce buds—and nipping bark if the snow is deep. They actually suffer from malnutrition and are in poor shape.

Come spring rains and warm sun and the deer begin to browse on hillsides and shortly become strong again. They feed on buds, ferns, moss, and clover and begin to feel frisky. They run and get in shape.

By the time hunting season comes along they are well fleshed out. They have stored up a bit of lard for the winter. They are in peak condition; the best condition they are going to be in all year. And if the bucks are in rut, they are feeling higher than in super shape. They're randy, rambunctious, strong, and just full of piss and vinegar.

And what about you? Had a nice summer? Drank a lot of beer? Sat around on weekends, sunning yourself or playing an easy round of golf while the deer were cavorting on the hillside?

Mister, if you aren't in shape to dog a mountain buck and follow him for 15 miles, then walk out of the woods and be ready to do it the next day, and maybe the day after, and maybe for a week, then just be an armchair buck hunter. Don't go out in the woods and kill yourself.

You've got to be in good condition to track down the trophy buck. By that I mean you have to have stamina. Get rid of that flab around your belly. Strengthen your legs. Strengthen your heart-lung system.

The biggest killer of deer hunters is the heart attack. An unconditioned body, larded with fat, filled with cigarette smoke, gas fumes, and softened by easy living, is not going to function while running after a buck. Mix poor condition and exhaustion with a dose of adrenaline when you see a buck, and you have a ticket to drop dead in the middle of the woods. Just hope your buddy finds your body. It's a helluva way to go, and it would be all your fault. I am particularly talking to middle-aged men, but even youngsters have to get in shape. My son, Lanny, is 28 and strong. Two years ago, he was scouting new buck range in Maine and in one day cruised the mountaintops and came out 45 miles by road from where he started. The last buck he killed in Maine he tracked for an estimated 23 miles, up and down mountains, between 10:30 and 4:30. On my 13 day deer hunt (Chapter 7), I tracked that buck and walked in and out of the woods, going to and coming from the track, over 300 miles. You need to be in condition.

I'm 50 and I can feel that my pistons are beginning to weaken. It just means you have to spend more time getting in condition. During the summer I'm a carpenter. Most of my work does not require hard physical labor. I exercise in the morning, at lunch time and in the evening. I do sit-ups, push-ups, chin-ups, deep breathing exercises, leg rolls and half knee bends. Mostly I am exercising my legs, particularly the thighs that take most of the punishment climbing and descending mountains. I also run five miles a day to give my heart and lungs a workout. If I'm tired, I know I'm doing my body some good and I keep working at it. Last summer, after eight weeks of conditioning, I could draw in the carpenter's apron four notches. I'm fortunate in that I don't smoke (I do like a good chew of "Red Man.") so my lungs are strong.

I go on a diet, if I'm slightly overweight, and avoid carbohydrates. I drink skim milk and, if you believe it, eat a lot of canned baby food for desserts and vegetables. They are very low in fat. I drink a little wine, but no beer.

Now each of you can work out your own level of conditioning. Some of you may do well to walk when you can drive, and walk upstairs and downstairs instead of taking the elevator. You can do isometrics with your thighs and stomach and shoulders while working at your desk or even while you are on the can. Jogging is very good for the whole body. So is bicycling. Nothing, though, beats walking or hiking in the mountains on the weekend, getting the feel of rough terrain under your feet and putting the legs and lungs to work as you hustle up and down hills. It's the best.

Bird shooting in the fall is great exercise. I do a lot of it, going after partridges with my .22 automatic. It helps me get in shape, and it also helps sharpen my hunting, for I like to sneak up on those partridges, locate them in the bush, and shoot their heads off (I also take a few of them on the wing). When you sneak up on a partridge, you must use the same stealth you use when you're pussyfooting up on a feeding deer. Try that for exercise too. Try walking through the woods for 200 yards and take a half hour and not make any sound. You'll find it's hard work, and you learn to balance your body in slow motion.

Bird hunting can do much for you if you do it regularly. My colleague Peter Miller, the fellow who helped me write the book (we call him Tanglefoot because he makes so much noise in the woods), is a woodcock hunter and uses a Brittany Spaniel. He hunts a few hours each day and cruises covers, sometimes in a rush, looking for flight woodcock. By the end of the bird season he is in shape too, except he smokes so much he ruins it all.

Come November you should be trim. Your lungs should be expanded, your heart should be used to doing some extra pumping, and your thighs should be taut. You should take care of your feet. Get them used to treading over rough ground. You don't want them all swollen and bruised from lack of use. If you have calluses on your toes, get rid of them. There's nothing worse than to be in the woods six miles and crack a callus and have it painful and bloody and then have to walk out. It's no fun. I know, because it happened to me.

Yours eyes and ears can get out of condition too. Put them to use. Try spotting things when you walk in the woods—look for chipmunks or birds, or pretend there is a deer peeking at you through the trees and with your eyes take away the underbrush piece by piece. If you bird hunt, and you have a dog on point, try and locate the birds on the ground with your eyes. Use you ears. Listen for small noise. Listen to silence. Get them working, for even at the keenest, they are no match for the Whitetail buck.

What I'm telling you is, build up your body and your senses for the hunt. Be in keen tip-top shape, for that deer will always be in better shape and stronger than you. Remember, that buck has four legs and you're tracking him down on his home ground.

Also work on your brain. Anticipate the hunt. Read about hunting, practice snap shooting or do some plinking. Be enthusiastic. For when the hunt comes, you want not only your body but your senses and your mind to be sharpened towards that one goal that will always be before you—bagging the biggest buck of your life.

—3—
CLOTHING

When you are on the track of a trophy buck, you are always moving. Sometimes you run, sometimes you trot. You walk, you range, you pussyfoot, just like the buck you are following. It's very important to be dressed correctly—not overdressed so you get all sweaty and exhausted, not under-dressed so you freeze. On your feet you need boots that will keep you warm, but also will allow you to step right out and, most important, to sneak quietly up on a feeding or sleeping buck.

I've run across human tracks in the woods that were big enough to be an elephant's imprint. I found out that some hunters wore oversized, space-type insulated packs. The boots were so big and so clumsy a deer would hear him cracking through the woods a hundred yards away. These types of boots are also heavy and will wear out a hunter. A tired hunter will lose that keen hunting sense that helps him get his buck. A hunter wearing these boots will walk a few hundred yards into the woods, get all sweated up and tuckered out and end up warming a stump, hoping someone will drive a deer into him. He can't begin to track a deer.

My sons and I wear light rubber boots. They are American made, and we buy them in any sport shop. They are similar to the type B.F. Goodrich makes. They are not insulated and do not have much support built into them. The important fact is that they should fit well. They should go on just like a glove. The reason for this is that you want your foot to be sensitive when you are pussyfooting up on a trophy buck. You want to be able to feel with your toes any branches that might snap once you put your weight on them. If your boot is so heavy you can't feel what's underfoot, you'll make snaps and cracks and that crafty buck will be roaring through the woods and you won't ever know it. Your feet should be light as your hands are when you caress a woman. Light boots make all the difference.

I prefer to wear two pairs of socks, a light wool pair and a medium weight, close knit wool hunting sock over that. I don't use felts, although many people do. My son Shane, who has poor circulation in his feet, uses felts and they help him quite a bit when the temperature is down to zero.

I pick a pair of boots that never squeeze the foot, but never allow the foot to move around in the boot. If the boot squeezes the foot, your circulation won't be working correctly and your feet will become cold and uncomfortable, and you forget about hunting. If the boot is too big, you will walk sloppily through the woods, your foot will slip more, and you won't be able to feel those noisy branches until it is too late.

When I buy a new pair of boots, I try them on both feet. I put on the socks I will wear in the woods, and then try on a dozen boots. My left foot is slightly smaller than my right foot and this means I try boots on both feet. Sometimes I find a pair that fits me perfectly, but often I have to match up a pair. Once I went through a dozen pairs of size 8 boots, mixing up the pairs even though they were the same size, before I found two boots that snugly fitted both my feet. You will find difference in sizes in different pairs of the same size from the same manufacturer. You may also find that a particular brand of boot just won't fit your foot. Then you have to look for another brand. I find it's best to buy my boots from a store that has a large supply of several brands so I can try on enough pairs to get a good fit. I also make friends with the sales clerk. Otherwise, he may think you are some sort of nut, trying on so many boots, mixing up pairs, and will try to hurry you out of the store. Explain what you are doing and take your time. It's that important.

Sometimes I use long underwear made from cotton but usually I don't. I just move so much when I'm on the track that long underwear makes me too hot and sweaty. Again, this is a personal preference. You might prefer long johns and your body may need them.

Always have several pair of everything you wear. If they get wet—boot and clothes—they might not dry out by the next morning. Also your socks and other clothes should be clean so they let the air circulate. If they become fouled with too much body sweat, the deer will be on your scent faster than they would if your clothes were clean. Even though I don't pay much attention to scent in the woods, I do know that buck don't care at all for sweaty man scent. Clean clothes make a difference. Although I do know some of the more successful hunters are backwoods farmers. They smell just like a cow when they go after their annual supply of venison, and I swear the bucks like the smell so much they walk right up to them.

I wear wool pants. Some of the hunting pants are straight falling. I blouse them into my boots, just as soldiers do. Otherwise, the bottoms will become wet, soggy, heavy, and soon frayed. If they are wet, they will freeze if it is cold enough. Frozen cuffs are heavy and noisy.

I also have had several pairs of trousers custom-made so they are pegged at the bottom. This makes them easier to blouse when you tuck them into your boots. I do not care for the jodphur type of hunting pants because they are cut too tight and do not allow you legs to move freely. This is important when you are climbing a steep bank. These pants will bind your movements. They will not allow air to circulate, and you'll become too hot, start sweating, then shiver with cold, and you'll forget all about why you are in the woods.

I wear a cotton T-shirt to soak up sweat and over that a light wool or cotton "chamois" type shirt that is sold by L.L. Bean, Herter's, and most sport shops. It is cut loosely to allow freedom of movement.

Over the shirt I wear a wool jacket. I have used one manufactured by the Johnson Woolen Mills here in Vermont. The Johnson jacket has a double thickness on the shoulder, which gives extra warmth and keeps me dry when it is snowing or raining. These jackets are loose cut and don't bind when you are snapping your rifle to your shoulder on a running buck. They have wide cut pockets which I like. It makes it easy to store my lunch.

On my head I wear a wool hat with a brim all around it so it can be pulled down to keep snow and rain out of my eyes and off the back of my neck. The one I use does not have ear flaps. I don't like ear flaps. I want to hear in the woods, and you should too, if you want to bag that trophy buck. But if you have a problem with cold ears, buy a hat with ear flaps, then cut away the flaps so they only cover the tops of your ears, but leave your hearing apparatus unobstructed. You'll find this method will keep your ears warm.

For gloves I use those brown cotton types that are lined inside with red material. They are light and warm and never catch in the trigger guard. I usually will buy a half dozen pair during a season. They easily become wet and I like to start the morning's hunt with a nice dry pair of gloves. These gloves can be found in just about any clothing store and are very inexpensive.

Now, you'll note that I wear nothing but wool for hat, jacket, and pants. The reason is that wool is quiet. It's silent and resilient, and it keeps you warm. What I wear is warm enough for me even below zero, because I'm always on the move. I might stop for a few moments, sometimes to eat, but often I eat when I'm tracking, munching on a sandwich or brownies, while I'm trying to catch up with my trophy buck.

The most controversial part of my hunting attire is that it is colored green. My boys and I wear green checkered pants, jackets, and hats. I have received more letters from readers of my articles complaining about this fact and how I will cause people to be shot and how, by advocating green, I am doing a disservice to the hunting fraternity. Some real dingbats wrote me some scathing letters. Unfortunately, these people did not read my articles carefully. I have never, never advocated the use of green in the woods. I have said only that my sons and I wear green in the woods. It is the way *we* hunt, just as this book is about the way my sons and I hunt trophy bucks. It is our method.

I wear green for several reasons. Years ago, when I was dressed in red, I was following a buck track through a beech grove high on a mountainside in Vermont, when I saw this hunter coming uphill. I wanted to let him know that I saw him. I waved my arm. What he did was bring his rifle to his shoulder and fire. "WHUCK!" That bullet plowed into a beech tree near my head. "Hey!" I yelled as loud as I could, I was so startled, and waved my arm again. "POW!" That son of a gun fired again and this time, I can tell you, I ducked pretty quick behind a big old beech.

I was young and the incident stayed in my mind. I decided then, that when I see a hunter, I don't want him to see me. Since then I have dressed in green and faded right out of the picture.

I can also wear green safely because I hunt in areas not frequented by other hunters. If they do come into my area, I know they must be good hunters to climb such mountains and they won't go gatling at every moving object. I also usually know when there is some hunter in my territory because in my morning swings on the side of mountains I will cut their tracks.

Everyone claims that deer are color blind and maybe they are. I have tied a red handkerchief to a tree and let the wind blow it to see if it would attract deer. I did the same with a white handkerchief. Both of them attracted deer about the same. This doesn't really prove anything, but I feel certain a deer can pick out a color that doesn't belong in the woods. If they are color blind, they certainly can differentiate between gradations of black and white. Green is a gray color on the black and white scale. Red is almost black. Fluorescent is quite bright. Now some hunter is stump sitting and there is a blaze of glory on his head and he is wearing fluorescent britches and a fluorescent cap and a fluorescent seat pad hanging down over his fanny and he uses fluorescent toilet paper and he moves about a bit, flashing it. All of the sudden, he grows horns and KABANG! he has a bullet coming at him. It's the same with deer. Bright shiny colors can attract their attention, but they usually take off in the opposite direction.

Green and black fits in with evergreens, white birch,

beech, maple, and other natural colors. I feel best when I blend in with the woods. I become part of the woods— I become a hunter.

Now, I would be a dammed fool and so would you to wear these colors in, say, New Jersey. You would be shot at before you could blink. It is also against the law to hunt without fluorescent colors in some states. In Maine it is against the law and the first time I hunted up there, I wore a fluorescent cape. It was made of some plastic material and when it was cold, the material became hard and made a racket when branches rasped against it. It also became brittle and cracked. If you hunt in a state like this, it might be best to buy a fluorescent cap, which Lanny has often used, or buy fluorescent cloth material and sew it onto the upper back, shoulders, and front of your hunting jacket.

I repeat—I wear green because I feel comfortable in it and I hunt where other hunters usually don't go. I would wear red if I felt at ease in that, but I don't. It is a matter of choice with me. I wear fluorescent capes in states that say you must do this, and if I was in an area crawling with hunters, I would wear fluorescent all over, you can bet your life. But you can also bet your deer rifle I wouldn't be hunting in an area crawling with hunters because I wouldn't very likely find any trophy bucks there. Those critters live where most hunters don't dare to go. And that's where you'll find me, blending into the scenery, tracking and a sneakin' and a peekin' after that old hoosier.

—4—
EQUIPMENT

I just can't believe some hunters. They are really
dressed to kill. They wear down vests under their
quilted hunting parkas. Their heads are buried under
fur lined hats with earflaps that tie under their chins.
Scarves swaddle their necks. Two pairs of pants and
oversized, elephant boots leaden their legs. The only
thing they can do is stagger to a stump. That's bad
enough—but then they really go overboard. They carry
powerful, expensive, and very heavy rifles with variable
power scopes on them. Ten-inch bowie knives hang
from their belts, so do 50-foot coils of rope which is
more than enough to hold several lynchings at once
rather than drag out a buck. Some of these nimrods are
weighted down with those long barreled, gunslinger,
single action .44 magnum revolvers. Cartridge belts
criss-cross their hips.

In addition, they carry flasks of bourbon, thermos
bottles of coffee, battery run socks, special hunting mit-
tens, fanny warmers, flashlights, first aid kits, and,
would you believe it, walkie-talkies so they can keep in
touch with the world.

Mister, I like gear and gadgets as well as the next fellow, and my house is full of them. But for God's sake,
when you are out in the woods, dress and equip yourself

for your main purpose—to track down and bag one big, oversized buck. Any extra weight or extra equipment is just going to bog you down and be a hindrance to the success of your hunt.

Be like an Indian. Travel light. Travel efficiently. Take what you need to succeed in what you are attempting to do and take no more. Pare your needs right down to the essentials. It is you against the buck. You should not be a walking display of a hunting catalog. Ask yourself—do you really need it? Why should a hunter strap a .357 or .44 magnum on his hip when he has a 7mm magnum on his shoulder? If you can't hit a buck with a rifle, you sure as hell aren't going to hit him with a pistol. Why would you distract yourself from tracking a deer by talking into a walkie-talkie? You'll squelch all the deer right out of the area. A 10-inch bowie knife is great for cutting firewood, but it will mutilate your deer when you dress it out. Booze and hunting never mix. Thermos bottles are heavy and you don't need anything hot if you are hot on a buck's track. At that time, you'll only want the sweetest elixir made on earth—a draught of mountain cold, diamond clear water, pure as the north wind, bubbling down among the rocks and boulders on a mountainside.

My equipment is selected to do the job, and no more. My dad, who was a blacksmith, made my knife for me when I was a youngster. It has a six-inch blade which I hone razor sharp. It has a thong handle which I wrapped with deer hide. On the brass hilt of the knife are notches that mark the number of deer I shot until I ran out of space. I carry it in a sheath I made that holds the blade and the handle. The sheath slips onto my leather gun belt, which I bought in a sport shop; it has 20 cartridge loops. And that is what I carry into the

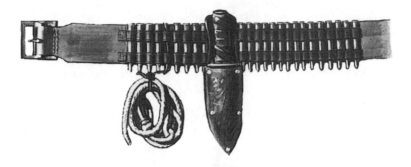

woods. I don't really need that much, but I feel more comfortable with 20 shells around my waist. Seems that I have better balance with them.

My dad taught me to wear a cartridge belt. If you carry shells in your pocket, they can rattle together and scare a buck away just as you are ready to shoot. My dad also taught me never to carry loose coins in the same pocket, for they jingle. He also taught me how to cock my old 45/70 so it made no noise. Even that click can send a buck scurrying away the split second before you shoot.

I carry a five-foot-length of quarter-inch nylon rope which is coiled and hangs from my belt. I have burned and melted both ends so they won't unravel. On one end of the rope I tied a slipknot and when I have a deer to drag out, I slip the loop over the antlers.

I carry a meager survival kit—two plastic envelopes of kitchen matches with their heads dipped in paraffin, another plastic bag filled with salt, pepper, and bacon grease in case I have to make an impromptu meal in the woods from a buck I shot. Sometimes I take along a pouch of bannock mix.

I do not use a compass because I am blessed with a sense of direction. I once tried to lose myself in Maine by not paying attention to the landmarks and after walking 15 miles, I still came out within two miles of camp. However, if I were hunting in flat wooded country, or land I was not familiar with, I would carry a topographic map and a compass. But you have to use the compass often and refer to your map if you choose this method to locate yourself. I prefer to use my eyes and head. Some people carry a whistle to alert others if they become lost. You can always signal with your rifle. Some carry first aid equipment, or cord to make a sling, crutch or lean-to. I never have, although it would be a good idea if you feel you need it to survive in the woods. I do take a few coins in case I want to mark my buck (see Chapter 10) or need to call from some gasoline station late at night to tell my sons to help me finish dragging out a 230-pounder because I am completely tuckered out. As my dad instructed, I always put the coins singly in separate pockets so they don't jingle. I carry a small piece of paper towel, which is a luxury, but can help you start a fire if you can't find any dry birch bark or dead wood, and a red handkerchief to mop up perspiration, sneeze into, or wipe my rifle dry. I also carry an empty plastic bag for the heart and liver of the deer.

For sustenance I usually take two sandwiches of cheese or peanut butter in plastic sandwich bags and brownies that my wife Iris makes that are extra rich in chocolate and give me energy when I am dogging a buck. My son, Lanny, sometimes totes a can of V8 juice and franks and beans, but I consider that just too much bulk. Each person will always vary their supplies to match their needs. The important point is that these supplies be light and functional. You should not pack any extra weight or gear that will impede your chances of bagging that buck.

The most important piece of equipment that you will

carry with you is your rifle. It is also the most personal, and the choice you make will be as much a part of your personality as your choice in a mate. You have to learn every part of that rifle. It must fit you well so that it aims where you shoot. You must learn its accuracy and the potential of its ballistics. I don't care what your favorite is—a 30-30, .300 Savage, a 7mm, or a .308, .270, or 30-06—a lever action, bolt action, pump, automatic, or even single shot—they are all good cartridges and rifles that will down your buck.

My first deer rifle was an old single shot .25 Stevens Crackshot. My second rifle was a Springfield 45/70 trapdoor single shot which my dad cut down into a carbine. I killed a number of bucks with both guns. My first real deer rifle that was not a hand-me-down was a .32 Remington Model 14 pump. I liked its weight and the way it handled. My third rifle was a .270 Remington 760

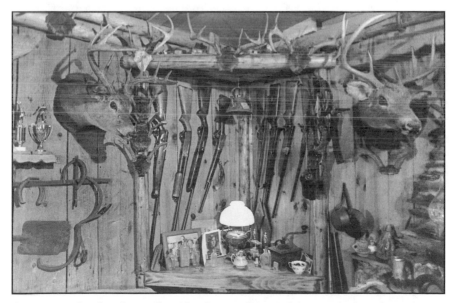

Some trophy bucks and retired guns in my home.

pump. After that I settled into the 30-06 Remington pump. I hunt in rugged country. When there is snow on the ground, I occasionally fall down, and snow can get into the action or gun barrel. There is nothing worse than to have a rifle jam when you have a trophy buck in your sights.

Lanny and I are partial to pumps. We feel they are the most reliable in all conditions. They are light and can take rough use and they are accurate. We use the Remington model 760 Gamemaster, and we like it fine. We have never had the Remington people offer us free guns or never have sought endorsements from them. That weapon is simply our choice. Through the years the Gamemaster has proven to be reliable and an old buddy to us and has knocked down many a trophy buck.

I pick my pump right off the rack. I look to see if the stock is well fitted; I try the action to see how smooth it is. I snap the rifle to my shoulder to learn its particular balance. Then I select the one I like best.

Once I am satisfied with the weapon, I go to work on it. I cut the stock down until it fits me as well as a fine made upland shotgun. Sometimes I have even lowered the comb so that it shot where I pointed it. The front sight I remove and replace with a Williams ivory bead that rides higher than the standard front sight on this rifle. The reason for this is that you want the bead to float high above the base so when you are sighting in on a running deer, part of the brush is not blocked out by a thick blade or a squat sight. You want the ivory bead isolated.

Then I remove the open sight and install a Williams peepsight. I remove the screw-in reticle and throw it away.

I feel the high front bead and peepsight is the fastest combination for shooting in the brush at running deer.

Most of my shots are within 100 yards and many times my target is a fast moving buck, crashing and leaping through the hardwoods. I know this sight combination well and I can see the brush and the deer and quickly find an opening in the trees where the buck will land. When the buck settles onto that bead, I touch it off. It is very important, I feel, to see as much as possible outside of the sight picture when you are swinging on a trophy buck who is skedaddling away from you just as fast as he can.

Now there are many hunters who are partial to scopes. If that is your choice, fine. But it should not be too powerful, no more than 2½ power when you are hunting in heavy brush. Out West, on the peaks or in the plains lands, you might want a more powerful scope, but in the East, I would say a 2½ power is maximum. If you do choose a scope, practice with it. Learn to find the sight pattern as quickly as you can when you snap the rifle to your shoulder. The use of the scope should become second nature to you. And remember, if it's snowing out, use pop up optical filters or you might find the scope lenses blurred by melted snowflakes or rain. With peepsights, you can usually just blow out any dirt, snow, or water drops. Personally, I think a scope can cost you your buck because it is so slow to pick up a running deer. It also raises the weight of your rifle.

Other hunters are partial to open sights, which I used for a number of years. These work well too, but I find that the older you are and the more your near vision deteriorates, the more difficult it is to keep the front sight centered in the notch. Also I find I cannot see enough of the brush when I am shooting at the moving target.

Peepsights are accurate. I can place bullet after bullet in the same hole with my open peepsight. The Remington 760 is accurate. I know, for I plugged a moose in Newfoundland at 400 yards—all three shots were centered in the rib cage.

During the season when there is snow on the ground, I circle the rear of the peepsight with red nail polish and also paint the ivory front bead red. This helps me to find my sight much quicker in snow or in bad light. Ivory beads are impossible to locate when you are in an awful hurry and the whole world between you and the deer is one big snowfilled scene.

I also install a Williams sling. These slings are carrying slings that make it easy to sling your rifle over your shoulder when you are dogging a buck. They are also very quick when you have to unsling the rifle and sight and fire in a few seconds on a fast disappearing buck.

Both of our Gamemasters are carbines. Mine has an 18 inch barrel. Lanny's has a 22-inch barrel which we cut down to 19 inches. The short length makes no difference. They are more accurate than we can shoot. It was with the 18 inch pump that I made the 400-yard shot on the moose. Lanny's longest shot on a Whitetail has been 200 yards.

The whole reason for the short barrel and the choice of the Gamemaster is because it is light and handy in heavy brush. The short barrel doesn't get hung up on branches. My gun weighs 6 pounds 13 ounces when loaded with five shells.

Sometimes we lighten the gun by removing the butt plate and drilling holes in the stock. In Lanny's rifle the holes helped to balance the rifle after we chopped off three inches of the barrel. Some people like to put matches and tinder or an extra round or two in these holes. Do so if you want to, but make sure it doesn't rattle and remember to carry a screwdriver to take off the butt plate.

I am partial to the 30-06. It has enough killing power for any big game in America and has a sweet trajectory so you can hold right on to your buck from 50 to 200 yards. I use Remington 180 grain Core Lokt cartridges, and they do the job. Lanny prefers the .270 for that extra speed and never has trouble shooting through brush. He uses 150 grain Core Lokt shells.

I like to personalize my rifle—give it a little more character than the Remington folks put into it—and I usually carve a deer scene on the stock, paint it with oils, then lacquer it. I also use brass studs to mark the number of bucks that rifle has knocked down. I tie a portion of a deer's ear onto the top of the sling. This is an old Indian custom. Deer have the keenest hearing of all animals and Indians tied a piece of deer ear on their bows for good luck.

Once I have finished customizing my weapon, I treat it with care, but I also use it, sometimes plinking, sometimes just shooting it to have the feel of it seep into my brain. It's good to keep in practice with you weapon. You shouldn't neglect it anymore than you do your wife.

This is our choice of equipment and firearms. Your choice is your own decision, and we all know that the old Winchester 94 lever action 30-30, which lots of people now laugh at, has killed more Whitetails than any other make of rifle or cartridge. A rifle becomes part of you, and whatever your choice, get to know it and learn how to use it, so that when you are at the moment of truth, and the trophy buck is lingering just a split second on your sights, that gun and you work as a team to bring home the venison.

—5—
SCOUTING FOR THE TROPHY BUCK

There's just one way you can hope to find your trophy buck, and that's to put your rifle on your shoulder and head out across the mountains. I've found there are two basic types of trophy deer—the swamp deer and the ridge runners. Swamp bucks have pointed, unscarred toes because they range and feed on soft ground. They grow big because swamps are easy places to hide; hunters don't like to muck through them, and visibility is often down to a few yards. I'm not a swamp buck hunter, but if I were, I'd probably arm myself with a shotgun, buckshot, and slugs for close-in shooting.

Ridge runners are my game. They are those big old bucks that, like the swamp deer, range in areas where there are few humans. Ridge runners keep to hidden basins and the mountaintops. Sometimes they will spend all but the coldest months within a few hundred yards of the mountaintop. Many a buck I've located has bedded down within a few hundred yards of 4,000 feet. They grow big and sassy and confident, for they know they are boss of their area. Their meat is sweet too, for they feed on beechnuts, mountain laurel, sweet birch (which is a delicacy to them), raspberry buds, and mushrooms, specially those that grow like scales on the sides of dead trees. They love fiddlehead ferns, which they paw for, even in November, scraping out the buds under a layer of leaves. This is good for those mountain deer. Their meat is succulent even when they grow old and huge. The oldest buck I have shot, as checked by a game biologist, was 10 years old. He was good eating too.

Another point: These mountain bucks are not used to being chased, and therefore do not run and flail their bodies as much as those pasture bucks, who spend much of their time dodging humans and being chased by dogs. Pasture bucks seldom grow to be trophy bucks. They live too close to civilization.

To find that trophy buck, you must roam the mountains. Go up high, right to the peak, and follow the ridge, zigzagging up and down, looking for sign. Look for nip marks, where deer have browsed on buds, berries, ferns, or whatever they choose to eat. Look for does. Bucks, of course, are often found with does. Keep looking for the trophy buck sign—their tracks, scrapings, pawings. If you don't find any good sign, well, take off and scout another ridge or mountain. Come back to that first area at a later date. You may find that some buck with a godawful big track has moseyed through.

The biggest reason why some people don't bag a trophy buck is that they hunt in the same place for two weeks. They have heard old wives' tales that the big ones are there. Usually, the case is that the big bucks in so called "hot regions" have been either shot off or moved out from the hunting pressure. Except for the occasional big buck who moves through when he's deep in rut, there are nothing but small runty deer that some hunters shoot and string up. They look just like oversized jackrabbits.

I don't know how many areas we hunt in a season.

Last year we hit at least eight regions in Vermont and Maine. When we find there are some nice sized deer in the area, but not trophy bucks, then we will hunt for a day or two and get out.

Lanny and I once spent a week in Maine, scouting for trophy bucks along the Allagash. We found nothing. The area was almost barren of wildlife. We left and motored south and saw in the distance some mountain peaks, and all glazed blue. They looked high. By that evening we were on the summit and had located some trophy bucks. In the next two days we each had shot our bucks, and both were over 200 pounds.

In mountain country the big bucks will always be up high, in remote areas. They seem to know most hunters are either too lazy, too weak, or too scared to go deep in the woods and high in the mountains and search them out. Last season, Lanny and Peter Miller scouted in Stowe, Vermont, a few miles from my home. Stowe is heavily hunted, but usually in the lowlands. Lanny and Peter climbed a 3,500 foot peak. The first 1,000 feet they climbed was laced with tracks of hunters, but there was hardly any deer sign. In the next 1,000 feet there were more deer tracks and little sign of hunters. Within 500 feet of the peak they found the sign of eight different bucks, two that Lanny estimated would go over 200 pounds. These eight buck tracks were interlaced within an 800 square yard area. Moving with them was a harem of does. Lanny estimated that the rutting season had ended, there was peace within the herd and they were hiding out on the ridge, waiting for the hunters below them to leave the woods at the end of the season. Lanny found no human trace in this region, which was three miles from downtown Stowe, one of the more popular recreational centers in New England and a region of which some locals like to say, "Aw, the area is just plumb hunted out. No good bucks a'tall."

You'll find your trophy buck if you scout the ridges. And what better way is there to get in shape than to do your scouting before the season, and find your buck's location?

You must remember this very important rule when you are scouting—deer range in circles. A while ago I was in a restaurant listening to a bunch of deer hunters. They agreed that all the bucks they ever chased never came back to the same place. "Why, he'll head right out of the country, lickety-split, and you'll never catch him there again. No sir!" I don't believe that at all. A deer is just like a big rabbit. Rabbits run in circles and so do deer, except they make a swing that might be 100 times bigger. I've put up deer and found that some will make a 10 or 12 mile circle. Often I've

Deer have nipped the buds from this mountain bush called Cat's Paw.

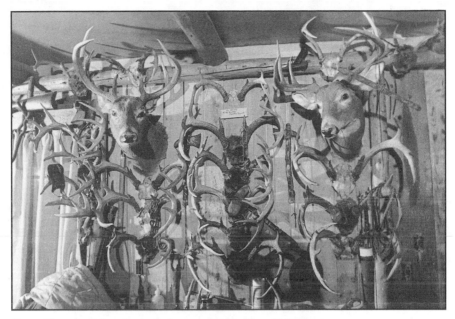

Scouting and hard work have paid off well for us.

jumped a buck from his bed, followed him all day, left the track at night and found him in the morning within 100 yards of where I first came upon him the day before. Some deer will range far—18 miles in a day. Others will make a small 6 or 8 mile swing. I've found that Vermont deer, for some reason, make a much bigger swing than the Maine mountain deer. Perhaps it is because the Maine mountain bucks are not as used to being tracked and trailed on mountaintops.

Your job is to break down that swing. You have to find out where the deer prefers to bed down, where the start of the swing is and where he travels during the night. Usually it will be along both sides of a ridge, or from a mountaintop down to a secluded basin and then back up to the mountaintop when it's beddy-bye time in the early morning.

It usually takes two days to break down the mountain buck's circle. In two days' hunting time, you should find out where the buck settles down and also you might run across the track of some other buck, possibly bigger, whose circle interconnects with that first buck's circle.

When we are scouting we will zigzag a mountain ridge to see if there is a buck swinging parallel to the ridge or heading down into a swamp or basin. But we, like deer, prefer to scout in circles. Lanny knows a spot, which he prefers to keep secret, where he says you can shoot the biggest buck of your whole life. It's an area where two ridges meet a stream, with heavy underbrush and good browse. It is on the highest part of a mountain ridge. Every time Lanny has visited that area, he has jumped a buck, followed him, and four hours later ended up where he started. I don't believe in stump sitting, but that's an area where you could plump yourself down and eventually get a buck.

There are many types of hunters, some who are good hunters, some who are bad hunters, some who are lazy, jealous, or just plain mean. But many hunters just don't know any better. The 100-yard hunter, for instance, will leave his car, walk one hundred yards into the woods, warm a stump, and wait for a deer to go by. He's the one I mentioned, dressed in flaming orange from tip to toe and carrying a 10-pound elephant gun.

The 200-yard hunter is a bit nervier. He'll head a little farther into the woods and park himself on a stump. Both of these hunters must like to hear the traffic go by.

Now the log road hopper just ambles up and down a log road all day long, and prays to God that someone up above will chase a buck down to him. Many times I've heard them walk by me when I've been trailing deer. I've heard them say, "Boy, what an area this is to see a deer come through!" They don't know it, but I have pushed a buck right by them many times and they have never seen the buck or me.

There are of course the car cruisers, who drive their rigs on back roads, drinking beer and looking for bucks. They really aren't hunters at all. On the other spectrum is the real hunter who is at home in the back woods, tracking and stalking his deer. Many of them hunt for their winter meat. They are the true hunters, and most are mountain men or farmers who just want some good sweet wild venison on their tables through the winter.

Many hunters become discouraged because they all hunt within a few miles of the main road. Most everything, as I said, within that range is shot or scared off. Actually there can be fantastic hunting a few miles further in.

The reason the deer are shot off in this area, and the reason that there are so many road hunters, stump sitters, and log road hoppers is, I believe, that most people are just plain scared of becoming lost. To be a good deer hunter, you can't worry about getting lost. That's when a lot of people lose their deer. They get anxious or they panic about where they are, or where they think they are, or where the car is.

A few years ago, Lanny ran onto a hunter who was sitting on stump, whittling with his knife. Every once in a while he would put his head up, just like a coyote, and yelp, "Helllllllllp!" He'd whittle some more, than give out with another yelp. Lanny leaned against a tree and watched him until finally the hunter spotted him and let out a frightful screech, as if he thought Lanny was a bear.

"Where'd you come from?" he said.

"Been standing here for half an hour, watching you," answered Lanny, "wondering what you're yelling about."

"I'm lost. Aren't you going to do anything about it?"

"I can't believe you're lost."

"By golly," the stump sitter replied, "I've been lost all afternoon!"

"The road is just over there 200 yards," said Lanny, and pointed.

"Mister," the stump sitter said, "I traveled in the area for an hour and I didn't find no goldarned road."

Lanny became a bit flustered. "Mister, you're lost and you're telling me there's no road over there? I'm not lost, you are—remember? I just came from there. You want to sit on that stump all night or do you want to follow me to the road?"

The stump sitter turned a bit belligerent. "There ain't no damn road over there! You're going to get me deeper into the woods!!"

"Stick your knife in that tree and I'll bring you right back to it after I show you the road."

"Yeah, and I'll lose my damn knife," the stump sitter mumbled.

Lanny snaked him to the road, pointed and said to him, "What's that look like?"

"Looks like a road."

"Sure it's a road."

"Where does it go?"

"It goes to town."

"That doesn't help me at all," said the stump sitter. "I'm still lost. I don't know where my car is."

"Mister," said Lanny, "what're you doing in the woods? This your first time deer hunting?"

"Oh no," said the stump sitter. "I've hunted for years."

"Yeah," replied Lanny, "and you must have been lost for years too."

Other hunters who think they are lost seem to lose all rationality. When we first hunted Maine some locals warned us about going deep in the woods. "You'll just get lost up there," they stated, "and them black bear will get you." I told these citified "Maniacs" that I wished the black bear good luck in our encounter, went where they told me to watch out, and shot my trophy buck. However, I believe some hunters must fear the timid black bear, or maybe the vastness of the woods, or perhaps themselves.

I was coming out of the woods one afternoon when a hunter, on a dead run, came towards me. Sweat was just rolling off of him and his eyes were bugged. He was running even deeper into the woods. I hollered and bellered at him, but he didn't seem to hear me, although he was only a few yards distant. I started tracking him and that poor devil finally made a circle and came out of the woods.

Another time I came across a man who was running. He practically kissed me he was so happy to see a human. He had been lost for two days, but had found a cabin to stay in. The cabin happened to be on the Long Trail, a well marked and used hiking trail that runs the length of Vermont. Didn't see how he could be lost on the Long Trail. He told me he had found a logging road but hadn't taken it for he had looked down the road as far as he could see and didn't see any settlement.

I told him if he used common sense, he would have followed the Long Trail, and bar that, all logging roads lead to headers, and where there's a header, there's a main road.

Lost hunters who panic could loose their lives through exhaustion of hypothermia. Naturally, they won't ever get their buck.

There are a few simple rules to follow. If you are one of those types who has no sense of direction at all, use a map and a compass. Analyze the map carefully. Refer to it. But better yet, do as Lanny and I do. Familiarize yourself with the terrain. In new territory we first climb the highest peak and take a look at the country. We memorize the mountains, ridges, draws, and basins. We also look for areas we think will be most fruitful in producing a trophy buck.

When we go into the woods and begin our swing, we keep our minds and eyes open. If we cross a small stream, we remember it. If we pass through a beechnut grove, or a sharp ravine, we put that into our noggins. We watch the sun. If we make a left turn with the sun on our left shoulder, we remember that too. When we first enter the woods, we might walk six miles in, then make a swing. If it takes three hours to walk in, it'll take the same to walk out, and that leaves you maybe four hours to make a swing or scout for that buck. Keep the sun in mind, or check your watch. Both will tell you when to leave the woods.

I was born with a sense of direction and have never been lost. I instinctively know where the car, or the camp, or north is. If you have done your scouting, you will find it is pretty difficult to become lost.

Now there are times I've been in the woods that I didn't know exactly where I was, but I never let it bother me, especially when I was on the track of a big deer. It just never entered my mind. When it became late, I just turned my nose toward the car and walked out.

It is hard to get lost. All small brooks lead to bigger brooks, which lead to rivers and roads. Logging roads lead to headers where the logs are or were loaded onto trucks. (However, in Maine a guy can walk his life away on some of those logging roads.)

If I hunt alone I always tell my family where I intend to hunt and when I expect to be home. If something happens—I break a leg or sprain an ankle—they know where to find me.

If you follow a stream, keep on the ravine above it, for you will find a mountain stream bed is filled with pools, boulders, and steep banks and make for very painful hiking.

Once I have done my scouting and have found a big buck's track, I don't just stare at the track. I look around, get to know that land and try to visualize on a mental map where the buck is heading, and where he is circling. I try to figure where he might like to browse the most—in the swamp, in the basin on fiddleheads, or in the beechnut grove just a few yards down from the summit. If it's a bad year for beechnuts, is that buck nipping away on birch and maple buds? I become as familiar with the lay of the land as I am with my rifle. Once I understand the terrain and find a good buck track, and figure out his swing, then I can say, "Mr. Buck, maybe not today, but tomorrow, or the next day, or the day after, you're mine." For I know that I will find his track each morning, back where I first picked it up, high on the ridge. And his stomping ground has become my stomping ground.

—6—
SIGN THE TROPHY BUCK LEAVES

The trophy buck leaves his calling card in a number of ways and it is up to you to recognize his calling card, for it will tell you as easily as if the old buck whispered in your ear—"Hey, I'm one helluva big buck—try to catch me!"

Naturally, the first thing you have to read and understand is the track. Is it buck or doe? If it's a buck, is it worth tracking for the next day, or perhaps the rest of the season, until you drop him? There have been times when I have passed up five buck tracks in a morning before I found one I thought was a big enough hoosier to go after.

You know, to tell a buck track at a glance is a gift that's very difficult to explain. Some people have it and some people will never learn. Once Lanny was called in by a friend to help sort out a "big buck track" that his friend claimed just disappeared. Lanny grabbed his rifle and went out to take a look, and just burst out laughing. His friend had been following squirrel tracks that disappeared when the squirrel scooted up a tree.

I started tracking deer when I was seven and just a whisker of a fellow living in northern Vermont. Tracking fascinated me. I even tracked dogs. I first started trailing bucks with my dad. He was a blacksmith, heavy of shoulder, a powerful man who loved to hunt and loved wildlife. He wouldn't kill anything needless. If we had any meat in the house, he wouldn't go out looking for it. That was the Indian in him, I guess. Dad was a marvelous tracker and people often wondered how my father could tell the difference between a buck track and a doe track when snow was on top of it. Yet he wouldn't tell me any of his secrets. I just learned, and when I told him what I thought I saw in a track, and I was right, his eyes would light up. I would search his face for the answer. Sometimes he would say to me, "There's a nice looking track, Ling," and I'd take it for granted that it was a buck track, and then I'd study it for all it was worth and try to figure out why it should be a buck. Dad's heaviest buck weighed in at 350 pounds. When I was eight, and hunting with him, he shot a 16-pointer.

It takes years of careful observation and lots of common sense to become a good tracker. I learned how a buck walked and a doe walked, on bare ground and in snow. I taught it to my sons. I have kept most of these secrets to myself and to my family, because I have found that a lot of hunters called me a liar when I told them. I guess that's human nature.

There are signs the trophy buck leaves for you to read. Probably eight out of ten hunters think that dew claws tell the difference between bucks and does. Well, does have dew claws too. So do pigs, for that matter. When does run, their dew claws will spread out just like a buck's. What you can tell by dew claws is the weight of the deer—not when it is running but when it is walking. If the deer is heavy, the dew claws will be well etched in the ground. Dew claws can be circumstantial evidence pointing towards a buck, but if you follow a track with large dew claws, you might surprise yourself to find your gunsights locked onto a great big bald-headed doe.

Lots of people say that a buck will drag his feet more than a doe. Bucks and does both drag their feet, particularly big does. You need a couple of inches of snow to tell for sure, for a big buck will drag its feet just a hair more than a doe. Drag marks aren't the best way to tell a buck.

There are many ways you can confirm a buck track, but when you are after a trophy buck, look for two important points—the weight of the deer, as seen in the hoof print, and the pattern of the track.

To tell the weight of the deer, see how deep the dew claws and the hoof print sink into the earth. If there is snow, brush it off and feel with your bare fingers the outline of the track. If the hoof sinks deep into the ground (Often the ground is soft under a layer of snow.) and is splayed, you can bet your life it's a big deer, and chances are it's a trophy buck. You take a deer over 200 pounds and you'll find there's no difficulty in tracking a deer like that. His foot really leaves an impression—on the earth and in your brain.

If the ground is bare, see how deep the hoof cuts into the leaves. A trophy buck's hoof will cut right through the top leaves. Compare that track to your own and take into consideration your weight. Compare the track to

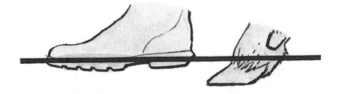

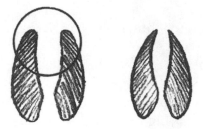

other deer tracks in the vicinity, or to your past experience of tracks you have followed that have led to a buck you have seen or shot. This will let you know quite a bit about the size of the deer.

Take another gander at that track. Really squint at it. A buck that lives in a swamp has long toes that are pointed, as there are no rocks or ledges. Mountain bucks often have stubby toes that are rounded or jagged, because they have been worn while that deer humped over rocks and ledges. It's plain old common sense that tells you a track that is jagged but well rounded isn't from a young little lightweight buck. It takes a few years for a buck to develop his track, and there's as much difference between a trophy buck's and a young buck's track as there is between a man's and child's hand. There's also as much difference between a buck's and doe's track as between your gnarled old hands and those of a woman.

A trophy buck's toes are more rounded. A trophy buck's tracks will spread out more than others, and really squish into the muck. But some deer are just like people. The have awful big feet, and don't weigh anything. Small deer with big feet have toes that don't splay out. Common sense tells me that a big deer track, eight times out of ten, means a big buck.

From these signs you should be able to tell the big

Not a trophy buck track, but he'll go 175 to 185 pounds.

The track of a trophy buck. He'll go over 200 pounds.

deer track from a small deer track, but you still aren't certain whether it's a trophy buck or just some monstrous doe that's trying to fool you. Now to really tell the difference, look at the pattern of the track. Look at tracks—not a single track, but a number of tracks—and figure how that deer sets his feet down—how that deer actually walks.

A very small deer, doe or buck, will often leave an even pattern of tracks, one track following the other almost in a straight line. A doe leaves a track in a fairly straight line; it's the way they are built. But one of those big trophy bucks, one of those long legged monsters who has heft and is broad of beam—built wide on the haunches— his tracks are staggered right and left. That's one of the strongest signs you can find for recognizing the big trophy buck. It's a sign you should never miss, and if you do, well mister, maybe you should be spending most of your time on the skeet range.

Deer amble, meander, walk, range, and run. Take a close look at the gait. A small deer takes small steps. That fact stands to reason, but many deer hunters don't seem to remember these reasonable common sense facts. Does take dainty steps, as my son, Lanny, says, just like a teenage girl at her first dance. Now a big trophy buck—he strides. That buck lopes along, and if that track has a big gait, you know there goes one big deer. If there is snow on the ground, small deer will sort of play hoppity, skippity, jumpity through the snow. Your trophy buck does none of that—he slogs through the mush with an even gait—he has the height and the strength.

What if the deer is running? Look at the track he's left. Big, 20-foot bounds between tracks means a big deer. When a big deer is moving down a mountain like a freight train, the distance between bounds can be even greater. If the ground is chewed up something awful where the running deer set down his four hooves and took off, you can bet your last cartridge that, considering the sign you've already read, you're on to one very big buck that's worth following.

When I see all these signs and the track tells me a buck is up ahead, strutting like a gander, God, I can feel it in my bones. I know it in my brain. It's just there. And it's a big one, my gut gets churning and I just want to set right after him and track him right down. Oh, a good buck track just sets me to quivering!

Now if for some reason you still aren't sure that you have a trophy buck marking up the world in front of you, track the deer for a few hundred yards. Again keep a close eye on how that deer walks through the woods. A doe will meander all over the place, just like a woman on a shopping spree in a department store. The doe will flit here and there, feed a bit, circle a tree, go under a fir and dilly dally around, just like a filly at the local Saturday dance. The buck won't. A buck will follow a much straighter line, and if that is a trophy buck sporting a mighty big rack, he won't be caught ducking into thickets or under fir trees. He's mighty proud of that rack and he'll circle all the obstacles that could tangle with his antlers.

When you see rubbings—where the buck has scraped his antlers on a tree—you know for sure that he is a buck. A buck scrapes and hooks trees for several reasons. His head itches at the base of his rack, like you back does sometimes, and he rubs it. A buck can be in rut, and he will hook trees and brush just to show his virility. And a buck, when he's angry, particularly if you are hot on his trail, will take out his frustration by hooking trees and brush. Another buck can make him do that too. Where he hooks and scrapes trees can also tell you how big he is.

Stands to that old measure of common sense that a trophy buck will scrape or hook a lot higher than some runty buck. It is also a fact I have seen a number of times that a big buck will have a favorite tree he likes to bang the hell out of, year after year. They will rip that tree into shreds, show off, and prance around. You can read the sign in the snow and on the bare ground. Take a careful look where that buck attacked the tree. If the scars on the tree are a day or so old, you know it's the same deer. Trophy bucks develop routine habits. And if that rubbing or hooking is off the ground three to four feet, mister, you're on to one big trophy buck that just ought to make your heart pound and your belly squirm, you should be so anxious to get him. If the rubbing is higher than that, you just might be onto a moose or elk.

Bucks paw the ground too; they also hook the ground. When they are in rut they often have only one thing in mind, and they're horny and belligerent. They'll paw the ground when they scent another buck. Then they get stiff legged and tippy toed, as they move up to the other buck, ready to have a grand go at it. A buck in rut will most often paw the ground where it is level. A feeding deer, buck or doe, often paws on a slope, look-ing for fiddlehead ferns or mushrooms that are buried under leaves or snow. Remember this—a feeding deer paws a lot deeper than a buck in rut will.

There's another thing bucks will do when they're expressing their manhood by scraping up mother earth. They'll paw the leaves something wicked, sometimes scrape up a few square feet, turning over the top leaves so the dark, wet sides are showing, then urinate in the leaves. Mister, don't be proud. Put your nose right down there and take a whiff. If it is strong, he was there in the morning. If it is faint, it is a day or so old. Be like another buck. He's leaving his calling card for does and bucks alike. And for hunters too. Think like a deer.

All these signs can be read in snow and on dry ground. When there is snow, the job is easier to read the sign. When the ground is bare, it is more difficult. If the leaves are damp, say from early morning frost or from rain, it's a lot easier than when the woods are dry. Then you have your job cut out for you.

A buck will often piss while it's walking, leaving yellow drops marking the snow. A buck, excited by a doe in heat, will leave urine marks 4 to 6 feet long. A doe leaves a big round hole were it has urinated. A buck invariably urinates when it passes another deer track—buck or doe. I have seen this sometimes 15 times a day. And a buck, if it gets a whiff of a doe in heat, will follow the doe's track. Curiously enough, a smaller buck will often follow a larger buck's track. Maybe the reason is somewhat similar to a young gunslinger going after the old pro.

A buck will often stick its nose into another deer track to get a good scent, and if there is snow on the ground, you will see the dimple where the nose was imprinted. If there is a good six inches of snow on the ground, you might even see the imprint of his tines and read how many points this particular buck has.

If you find where the deer has bedded down, give it

a very careful eyeballing. A trophy buck doesn't curl up into a ball like a doe or small buck—he lays right out and stretches himself over the ground—he's just too big to do any small curl up when he wishes to take a snooze. If there's snow on the ground, take another close look. I mean really close. Look sharp, because you ought to be able to see the imprint of his antlers in the snow and maybe the spread of the antlers. Two years ago in Maine I knew I was onto what I thought was a 14-pointer by seeing seven tine marks in the snow. He ended up a 13-pointer.

There are so many ways to tell a big buck track that it seems impossible for me not to know what I'm after. But it does take a lot of experience to tell the big buck track—the deer that goes over 200 pounds. However, if you keep snooping in the woods, remember what you saw, for you'll gain the experience to tell the 200 pound-plus buck sign. It may take seasons of roaming the woods and keeping your eyes peeled and your brain sharp, but that's what trophy deer hunting is all about. Rely on your eyes, your brain, your memory, and your common sense, and you'll bag the big buck, sure as shootin'.

−7−
ON THE TRACK

Now that you have spotted the big buck's track, and you know it's not only a big buck but a rangy, crafty critter sporting an awesome rack, and he's out there in front of you, you also know it's time to track him down. The most enjoyable part of the hunt begins—trailing the trophy buck.

You must have only one thing in mind, and that's bagging that trophy buck. Don't be thinking about your wife and the milkman. Don't worry if your car is going to start when you come out of the woods after tramping 20 miles. Don't worry about getting lost. Don't fret about if the cartridge is going to go off, or whether the firing pin is broken, or whether the rifle sights were bent the last time you fell down. Don't get anxious about pulling a muscle. And never get sick of chasing this buck, for when you begin to have those thoughts that buck will walk circles around you and you'll never see him. When I set on a track, I wonder if he's as big as I think he is. I say to myself, "That fellow must have some antlers by the imprinting in the snow . . . I want him! You got 14 days left, Mr. Buck, and if I haven't downed you by then, you're one smart buck." When you are worrying, you are no longer hunting.

Turn on your senses when you are on the track.

Tune into the woods and the mountains. The hunting scent is in the air and every move and everything you hear coincides in stalking your deer. If you don't turn yourself into a hunting animal, you won't get that buck.

The first thing you have to be sure of is which direction your buck is moving. This may sound foolish, but in deep snow, if you don't study the track closely, you may end up tracking that buck in the wrong direction. Feel with your hand if the track is snow covered, and find the outline of the toes, then you know for sure. A while back I was coming down a mountain in northern Vermont into a large basin, and I spotted the track of a large deer moving up the mountain. It had been made during the night. There was about eight inches of snow on the ground.

As I walked further down the side of the mountain, I cut onto this hunter's track, which was following the deer track down the mountain. So I followed both tracks and down a ways I came onto this hunter. I hollered at him and asked him if he was following the deer track.

"Yeah," he said, "what's it to you?"

"Nothing," I answered. "It's no skin off my nose."

So I followed along behind him and then said to him, "You're really following this deer?"

"Course I'm following it! Don't it look like it?"

"Yeah," I told him, "it looks like it, but are you trying to find out where he was born or where he is right now? You're trailing him backwards, you know."

"Mister," he said, "I'll have you know I've been trailing deer and tracking deer all my life and I don't need no smart upstart young punk telling me how to track a deer."

"Sorry I mentioned it, and have good luck, my friend. You might get him tomorrow, or the next day, if you backtrack him," and I left him. As far as I know, he's still tracking him. If a hunter who has been tracking all his life can't tell the difference between a forwards track and a backwards track, then he might as well quit doing it. Deer can only walk in one direction at once, and it was pretty obvious that this particular deer was going uphill, heading into the mountains. If I'd have come on the track sooner, I'd have tracked him down.

Now you know for sure where that deer is headed, but you still have to answer a few questions. What is that buck's range? As I stated in Chapter 5, all bucks range in circles; they are just like big rabbits. You have to break down that circle the deer follows. You have to know how far he is in front of you, for that buck might have an 8 hour jump on you, and maybe more. You might trail him all day and never see him, and you might pick up his trail the next day, kick him out of his bed within the next hour, or maybe not catch up to him until late in the afternoon when it's time to leave the woods. If you find the buck makes a complete circle in three or four days' time, and you know where, that buck is your buck. Many times we have shot our bucks before they completely made their swing. It depends upon how hard we're pushing, how fast the buck is moving, whether he is in rut and has located a bunch of does, or is marching off somewhere else looking for strays, or whether he is just ranging and feeding, or whether he is just a sly, fast moving devil that likes to play tricks on you.

Now you have to learn just how old that track is. If the track is on dry ground, take a look at the leaves that the deer has turned up. Are the back sides all dried out compared to leaves that have not been disturbed? Have dirt and leaf fragments crumbled into the track? If the track is clean and the leaves look freshly turned up, you know that buck is not far ahead. If the ground is wet, how much muck has collected in the track? How does it compare to your own track? If there is fresh snow on the ground, dust it off from the track and eyeball the outline of the track. If the track is hard and rigid it's at least one day old. Frostlines in the track can also mean it's a day old. But if the snow in the track is granular and you can move it around in your hands, the track may be a few hours old.

When there is snow on the ground and it is warm, don't get fooled. A melted out buck track may look like a whopper but could be a small 110 pound deer track. It only takes about an hour for the sun to beat down and spread out that track. Look for the outline of the original track. You may find the actual track is one half inch smaller than the outline. If you know how long the sun has been beating on the snow, you can guess the age of the track.

There is a lot to reading the age of a deer track that should be spewed out by that computer in your head. Much of it is past experience, but you should keep current weather conditions in mind. Deer move at night and bed down in the morning. What was the weather like the day before? If is was warm and mushy, then cold overnight, and snowed a few inches, you should be able to tell to the hour when that track was made.

Is that buck traveling with a doe? If there is one doe with him, chances are you are going to get a shot at him. But if that buck is traveling with a group of does, nine times out of ten all you will see are the does, and your buck will be off loping to one side. It's best to split a buck away from his harem, which will happen anyway if you are on his track. Does are fickle and they will pack up and run quickly if they find their stud has the misfortune to have a good tracker dogging right after him.

Now you're ready to track that buck and find out a lot more about him. Your mind is set right. You have nothing to worry about except that buck. Now forget about your scent. The winds blows in four directions, and sometimes in all four at once. If you worry about your scent, you'll never move fast enough to get that buck. A plus here is that deer are curious. Sure he'll smell you. But if you stay on his track, he'll get curious, angry, or both. He's going to stop, or backtrack, to get a look at just what is following him.

There's another thing you do here. You might not get that buck on the first day, and will have to pick up the track the next morning. Try to recognize that buck track. I have tracked bucks that have had a broken hoof, a limp, or in one case, a rear left hoof where the right toe was ingrown more than it should be. Plant his signature in your brain so you can sort him out anytime—if it's the next day or after he's walked through and circled a herd of other deer that could include other bucks. (Sometimes, you might find a bigger buck track than the one you are following. Then I switch, naturally, to the bigger buck.)

There is a time to run or dog a deer, a time to trot, a time to walk, and a time to pussyfoot.

If the track is old and you know that deer is hours ahead of you, sling your rifle and trot right after him. Noise and smell make do difference, just get on his trail. Pretty soon you'll know what that deer is doing. He might be in rut and looking for does and moving all over the place. At times like this he won't be feeding much. Sometimes bucks range—just trotting right along. Then is the time for you to jog right after him. Keep your eyes

open for other signs too. As I said before, if your buck has pawed the ground and urinated on it, you can smell the urine easily. But if the odor is faint, it could be a day old. Has that buck shredded a tree? Check the scar he's made. Is it fresh looking? How about the shreds of bark on the ground? Are they fresh? Is the underside of the bark fresh or has it darkened? Are the shreds curled? If they're not, that deer could be closer than you think.

When that buck you're trailing moves from a trot to a walk, you move from a trot to a walk. When he stops to browse, nipping buds here and there, mister, you better be on your guard, then it's time to start pussyfooting for chances are that buck will browse just a bit, then bed down. It only takes a buck about an hour to browse and bed down.

During the deer season I have found that bucks usually don't have more than a few pounds of browse in their stomachs. They don't eat much. Sex is on their minds, and their bodies are in excellent condition from stuffing themselves all summer.

When a buck is browsing and standing about, nipping buds, pawing for food, and eating mushrooms from the side of a tree, he may move just a few feet in a half hour. If it takes you one half hour to move ten feet, then take one half hour. If you make one mistake here, that buck will know it, and be off faster than you can blink, and you'll never see him.

When I start pussyfooting, I hunch down, glance at the track and where I can walk without making noise, and I keep glancing around. You can see at a 40 degree angle off to the sides and your eyes should be constantly swinging. Just because that buck is moving in a straight

line doesn't mean he can't be off to the side. Many times, when a buck is ready to bed down, he'll make a small circle uphill from his bed, just checking out the security. He may be eyeballing the back of your head from above when you're looking at his track up in front of you.

When you see by the sign that your buck is no longer browsing, then you know he is not more than 50 to 100 yards from you and you have to do more than just sneaking and peeking. You sort of flatten right out, hunch close to the ground. Many, many times I have been that close to a rangy old buck and he's won the game. He's there giving me the eye before I spot him, then he snorts and my hair curls and my heart stops, then spurts madly, and I just catch a glimpse of him tearing through the brush like a locomotive.

Well, the game is on again. I scold myself for being a dummy, sling my rifle and start right after him full bore. I run, literally run, after that bounding deer. If I have to run uphill, I run uphill. Sometimes, when I hit a crest of a peak, around 4,000 feet, I'll be coated with rime frost and look like some grizzled snowman. But I keep after him. When he slows to a trot, I slow to a trot. When he stops to feed or to listen, I do the same, and we play hide and seek, and sneaking and peeking. Now I hope to get him again.

Sometimes, I have to leave the track at the end of the day, and I'll pick it up the next morning. Hopefully, during the first day's hunt I'll have figured out part of his circle and the next day I'll hit the ridge and zigzag up and down until I find his trail and sometimes his bed. These old bucks, as I said, have habits, and they usually bed down in pretty near the same location, night after night, even when they have had a hunter on their tail. A long winded buck might take off with you after him for 18 to 20 miles, then that night return to his stomping ground, going as much as 40 miles a day. Remember, he has four legs, you've got only two.

Get to know the habits of that trophy buck you're tracking. If that buck is in rut, he'll be chasing down does and anxious to fight other bucks, and, just like us, he gets a little careless when he's excited. You can read all this in the ground. You can see where your big buck has chased a doe and butted her around and mounted her. Remember, the buck gets excited because the doe is in heat. He literally goes out of his mind. His neck swells, his pride gets high, he's randy and practically insatiable. If that buck of yours is after a fight and smells another buck, he'll walk stiff legged and take little sharp pointed steps in the snow. He'll bristle right up, walk on the tips of his toes, his head will go down, antlers out, and he'll bellow right from the bottoms of his lungs. It's an odd sound, and if you hear it, your hair will curl. You'll never forget the sound. Most times though, you only hear it, because you become anxious and make a mistake. I almost came onto a fight two years ago. I heard the sound high on the mountain—an awful racket. The buck I was following tore hell out of a smaller buck. The ground was literally ripped up. Spots of blood reddened the snow and the deer hair was everywhere. The smaller deer limped off, but I noticed he limped off at a run.

Some deer, after they know you are on their track, become awful curious as to just what it is that is bugging them. They will stop and look, sometimes a half dozen times. If you have a buck like that in front of you, you have a buck that isn't going to live very long. Other bucks will circle around you, and this is another reason to keep your eyes open to the side.

Sly old trophy bucks don't want you on their track at all. Some of them will just try to run away. Others will try to lose you by milling around in a yard of deer, including bucks and does. When this happens I generally follow the buck in and figure he'll come out of the yard in the opposite direction. Other times though, you have to circle the mess of tracks and sort out which one was yours, or which one is bigger. This is where it comes in handy to know your buck's track.

I've had bucks double back on their track and jump off, trying to lose me. Other bucks have followed streams and half a dozen years ago one did this to me in northern Vermont, following a stream right down the mountain. After a mile I thought I had lost him but on a rock I saw splashes of water and knew he was ahead of me. I tracked that deer right through a town.

Some other bucks I have tracked have followed other buck tracks, hoping to lose me. And many times, I have seen a smaller buck track a bigger buck. I have walked onto these smaller bucks, pointed my finger at them, said, "Bang! Now go away and grow up, little feller," and watched them, startled out of their skins, bound through the brush. Some of them were good bucks, but never as good as the one I was on.

I have followed trophy bucks that are ornery and mean. They are mad and frustrated at this thing that is following them and they will hook brush and the ground and trees and stamp their feet. Often those angry bucks spend too much time doing that and they suddenly find their rib cage is pinned to my sights.

Eight falls ago I was on a large buck track for five days. That old buck didn't like me on his track at all. He was some upset about it, I could tell, because he pawed the ground and hooked branches. He was belligerent and looking for a fight. I had put him up out of his bed on the fifth day and he roared down the mountain with me right after him. He forgot about me and rammed into three does, charging right after them. They took off to the left of a ravine, and the buck to the right. Then he ran into two does and a 7-point buck. That buck I was following just leaped down the mountain and in one mighty 30-foot leap rammed into the smaller buck.

I came on the scene five minutes later. The 7-point buck was just getting to his feet. I figured he had a broken shoulder and fractured ribs, the way he was breathing so hard. One eye was punched out and when he stood, his head was down, which is a sign of an injured buck. There wasn't much blood so I also knew the injury was internal. I knew he'd live, that poor old fellow, and I kept right after the big one. I finally nailed him—a 230-pound 8-pointer.

I never had a buck charge me, although Lanny has, on a deer he had tracked for several days in northern Vermont. That buck started charging from 30 feet away. Lanny, however, just loves to get gatling with his .270 and that buck didn't get too far. "Gosh, Pop," Lanny said to me as we dragged that animal out. "He sure surprised me. I figured he had more brains than that." The deer was an old, 215-pound hoosier with eleven points.

There are other characteristics about bucks I have tracked. Some are real skitterish of humans, and these are the ones found in the lowlands. Ridge bucks often have not had too much contact with people and are easier to track. Maine bucks, I have noticed, are not half as shy as Vermont bucks, and I think it is because they have not felt the hunting pressure. The bucks I am talking about, of course, are those high on mountains, where few hunters have dared to stray. I imagine that bucks in other states, such as Michigan and Pennsylvania and even Texas, all have different levels of wariness. And each buck that you track is different, just like humans. Some cover a lot of territory in their range while others prefer a shorter circle. Some are curious, some are ornery, and a lot of those big hoosiers are sly. You can spot them sometimes when they get out of their bed, their head low to the ground, streaking away like a comet. You often see pictures of deer bounding through the woods with their heads high. Bucks don't do that. They keep their heads down low.

Bucks are supposed to crawl on their bellies to hide from you. That sure is some buck tale. I've never seen a buck crawl on his belly when he could be making 25-foot leaps, putting a lot of distance between you and him. This is the same sort of tale as one I recently read—that a buck will rub his hind legs together to get the musk working from his scent glands. If you ever see one do that, lasso him and take him to a carnival, for he'll have to be some contortionist to rub his hinds knees together.

There's lots you will learn on the track, much you can figure out about all bucks and about the one you are following. You will also be smart to mind the weather. If there's fresh snow on the ground, and more snow falling, and there's little wind, and you find a buck track, you should have him before sunset. If the snow is frozen and crackly, the chances are against you. When the leaves crunch like cornflakes when you put your foot down, you might as well be home, for it takes mighty good luck to get a shot at a buck when it is noisy. The wind doesn't help either. Deer and all other wild game become very wary when the wind is up. You rarely spot a buck in this sort of weather.

But a good snow, even a blizzard, can't be beat. I and my sons have slogged after bucks in snow three feet deep (soft, fluffy snow, not three feet of wet snow) and there's no finer time to hunt than when the woods are freshened by a blanket of snow—the noise is deadened, the wind is still, and you know the bucks are moving. That's the best condition for hunting you'll ever find.

The buck that I tracked the longest was a wiley old Vermont ridge runner who ran the mountaintops in northern Vermont. He led me on the track for 13 days before I downed him. He was a smart creature and a noble one. I wrote about the hunt for *Sports Afield* and I am running it here again. Read it carefully, because that buck pulled most of the tricks I know. You'll learn a lot on how a buck thinks.

THE THIRTEEN DAY DEER HUNT

I knew he was up there somewhere, browsing about, up on that mountain I know so well. Last year I saw his sign a bit and had a peek at him. He wasn't a barrel chested deer—the type that look more like a buffalo with spindly legs—and he wasn't a lean or a long deer, he was just a well-built deer. He had a good pair of legs, he sure did. He was a good runner, a big mountaintop deer, living above 3,300 feet. I don't believe he came down during summer or winter, except when the snow was laid in deep. I think he lost his antlers up there too. You could lay a 30-06 cartridge in his tracks sideways and it wouldn't fill it and I figured he would go over 250 pounds. His rack was heavy, wide spaced, and very, very thick. He had 10 points and five years of mountain running. I planned to get him.

First Day

It was two hours before dawn when Lanny, my son, Uncle Windy and I drove north to the mountain and ridges that run parallel to the road that leads into Canada. I dropped Lanny off 18 miles from where I went in. He would work over the range and hunt six to eight miles from me, down in the swamp basin. We never hunt together until we have some cleanup work. Uncle Windy hunted down low and I was heading to the peak of the highest mountain. On the first day we were just scouting, looking for sign and I was looking for that big one. It was pretty black out that first morning, a slow wind whistled through the trees. It was damp and quiet walking—spongy. There was no snow on the ground but I knew there would be shortly, I could smell it, coming in with a soft wind from Canada. I walked straight up the mountain, about three miles in, up to the browse area where I thought I'd find my buck. There was good browse on this mountain: beechnuts, mountain laurel, maple, the tender shoots off birch. Birch is very sweet you know.

I was up near the top about 10:00, when small flakes sifted down, then changed to good heavy flakes—typical high mountain early season flakes—and the snow began sticking to the ground. We never lost the snow for the rest of the hunt. I had circled the area looking for sign, but with the snow coming down heavy I hunched under one of those scrawny spruce trees stunted by the altitude. They never have any body to them. I sat there, dry, warm, just waiting. I was about 3,400 feet and the mountain peaked out at about 3,700. I knew the deer would be moving in the storm in the afternoon, and I had lunch, brownies, a peanut butter sandwich. I met a friendly chickadee. He'd land on my finger and pick at my ring. I'd snap my fingers and he'd flutter up, scold me, then come right down and land in my hand and do it again. He liked brownie crumbs.

After lunch a couple of does trotted in sight. Nervous they were, fooling around. I didn't know why, but maybe there was another hunter below them—probably my son. They wouldn't stop to feed and kept looking back down the mountain. It was snowing pretty hard then and you could see about 75 to 80 feet. The blizzard was really setting in, and would drop about eight inches of snow that day. The storm was going full swing about one o'clock and I knew the deer would be moving and I started to move parallel to the ridge, zigzagging up to the summit, then back down, trying to find where the old boy would get up and start moving around.

I was walking slow, just more or less wasting time, and sure enough I came across his track. He was with a doe and I could see right off he was a big deer and I was pretty sure he was my deer. Those big deer, they have a home and they hang right into it. You know, there's a way to tell a buck track just by glancing at it. More people get fooled by dew claws or a splayed track, but all deer got dew claws. So do pigs and goats, and all deer with weight splay their hooves. To recognize a buck track right off, well, it took me years.

These two were just browsing several hundred feet off the summit; they had come out of the spruces on the top and were working down. They didn't know I was about so I started sneaking and peeking, because I knew he was right in front of me; I could tell by his tracks in the snow. And they were feeding slow, on buds, on short, sparse trees that up there are only two or three feet off the ground; you could see their nipper marks.

I was on to them for about a half hour when I felt eyes on me and I turned my head to the left. There they were, staring right down on me. The buck and his doe had probably been watching me for three minutes, just frozen up there, hidden by some spruces, peering at me through the snowflakes. They were about 50 feet uphill. They had zigzagged while browsing, moving uphill. Oh, he was a big buck. He was my buck all right, and I felt like killing myself because I missed him.

My rifle was ready but I never had a chance to fire. I saw antlers, a body, then he was gone. He went straight up and over the top. I called myself a dummy and all kinds of other things for a few seconds, slung my rifle, and took right after him.

I had been with him for about an hour and had dogged him right over the top of the mountain and down the other side to about the 2,600-foot level where I was below the snowstorm line and I could see good. He had slowed down, and wasn't taking those 30-foot jumps and I slowed down too and kept looking forward. I spotted him down about 90 yards.

I use a 30-06 carbine with an 18-inch barrel. I carved a big running deer on the stock, and it shoots where I want it to. I pulled my rifle up just as he broke into a run and I followed him, waiting for him to hit an opening and for that moment when he would pause with his legs all bunched up, ready to leap. He got into an opening, all bunched up, and I squeezed the trigger and at the same time a tree jumped right smack out in front of the sight. It was a 10-inch birch and I hit it dead center. I don't know how they do it, those trees, but most deer hunters have chuckled at that because it has happened to them many times.

The buck headed northwest, parallel to the ridge. He would run, trot, walk, browse, with me right behind him. It started to snow again and sometimes I could see no farther than 50 yards, but usually less because he and I were moving through thick brush. He was not following a trail but in typical buck fashion he was going where his feet happened to lead him. Oh, he knew where he was going all right, he knew the route but he was not following the trail.

And he knew I was there with him. He would cut up the mountain, then down, then back up again. He circled, twisted, and backtracked. He backtracked several times on his own trail to see if I was coming. I guess he was worried about me. He saw me several times, I could tell from his tracks. Sometimes he backtracked 50 yards. Backtracking is a mistake, because I catch them in the act and they find me in front of them, sighting down the barrel.

You see, a deer doesn't always trust his nose, they just have to backtrack and see what is following them. They don't understand—"What is that persistent thing behind me?" And if they're in rut, why, they make more mistakes, fooling with the does and battling other bucks. This one, though, wasn't in rut. His doe left him way back on the high mountain. In typical fashion does usually start packing their bags a few minutes after they are jumped.

The buck finally headed for a swamp, a big basin, and I left his track a little before dark and walked out on a log road to the main road and waited for Lanny or my Uncle Windy to pick me up. I figured I had dogged that buck 18 miles and I knew he was smarter than I first reckoned.

Second Day

I knew that buck would be back where I picked him up the first day so I went to the same area, up about 3,400 feet and zagged around and about 8:30 I found his trail. I knew it was him by the size of the hoof print in the snow. It was murky out, the clouds were low and dark, and there was a light snow falling when I started after my buck. An hour later I watched him rise out of his bed and walk away from me, right into the falling snow. He never ran. He was laying down in thick spruces, about 60 yards from me. I guess I let him go, I could have had him.

Well, then again I like to get one good shot into a deer, and I like to take my opportunity. I don't like half shots— never did—don't like shoulder shots or neck shots. I like rib shots, right into the boiler works. When you shoot them in the boiler works they go for probably 30 yards and are practically dead on their feet and they don't even realize it. I really didn't have that type of shot at him.

So I tracked him, and he began to play some tricks on me. He got into a bunch of deer where there were four or five does and tried to shake me onto another track. I saw sign where he ran into a small buck and didn't challenge him so I knew he wouldn't waste time with the does, or fighting other bucks. He must have walked into 15 different deer that day to see if he could lose me. He didn't and he worked northwest, the same direction as the first day. I followed him for about four hours. I was moving along at a good trot.

I let him go in the late afternoon, and walked down the mountain onto the road. I was working through the spruces halfway down when I ran across a fisher cat chasing a red squirrel. Fisher cats make the most vicious sound you ever heard when they are after any-thing, and that cat was trying to scare the squirrel to death. The squirrel was leaping blindly from limb to limb but the trees were small and the big cat couldn't get leverage and stayed about five or six feet behind the squirrel, screaming, till he saw me and took a powder. I've come across hedgehogs a fisher has killed. They run under a limb where the hedgehog is and open him right up across his belly, and that hedgehog is dead and doesn't know it. The fisher eats the hedgehog inside out and when he's done that hide lays right out like a rug. I found them in the woods—the only thing left is the upper part of the skull, the teeth, and the hide laid out just clean, no backbone or nothing. You see a fisher cat you want to be damn thankful you saw him, because they are rare and very evasive, just like the Whitetail I was after.

Third Day

At 8:00 I was onto his track again. Just like clockwork that devil would be right back in the same area. He was meandering and browsing slow like and I was soft behind him, slow and peeking. But he got me again. He whistled so hard at me, it practically knocked my hat off. Then he was off and so was I, trotting right after him. He would run, taking those 20 and 30-foot jumps, then he would slow right down. While he was running I would cover some ground too and I'd catch up with him right along. But I never saw him that day. I followed him for about five hours and all I saw was a smaller buck who was trailing my buck. It happens often. Altogether I ran across seven bucks who were trailing my big one. Some might be trailing out of curiosity, but in typical buck fashion they probably wanted to fight. I'd catch up to them, about 60 yards, sometimes a lot closer and I'd point my finger at them and say "Bang! I got myself another buck!" and let them go. Most generally they got a good look at me and they'd take right off in a heck of a fright.

Fourth Day

I saw him this day, about 80 yards in front of me, hidden in some brush, moving away at a trot. I didn't have a good shot, so I didn't fire. He was back in his stomping ground and although he got away, I felt a little more enthusiastic about killing him and I followed him again for 18 miles. He'd zigzag the mountain and ridge always heading northwest, going up to the summit, then heading back down, trying to shake me, but never going below 2,600 feet. He had his routine and I knew if he stuck to it, I'd catch him eventually. I also knew he was upset about me being on his tail. He wasn't in rut, yet in several places I saw sign where he tore hell out of the trees and the snow, pawing, scratching, banging away. He was getting to be just a bit frustrated with me, for I was always with him.

It was damp cold that day but I wasn't uncomfortable. I dress light because I do a lot of dogging and sometimes my hair and jacket get all rimed with frost when I'm on the trail. Sometimes I moved in close to him and I could smell him, the stink would linger because he would be running and sweating. I didn't see him again that day but he was sure learning my scent.

You know, with big deer, you got to be patient, because they are smart. You can say, mister, that this buck was smart, he proved it to me. I think he was one of the smartest I ever trailed. Just to get away from me he was smart. Normally I nail them right in their bed, and usually two days is about the limit I'll track a deer. Any more than two days and you know you are onto an exceptionally smart buck.

Fifth Day

I picked up his track no less than 50 feet from where I found him the day before. He had come back again, a round trip of 36 miles. It had snowed again during the night, and it was up to my knees. I was just easing along, it was early in the morning and I was bending down to check his tracks in that deep snow. While I was piling away the snow to look at the track, I heard a crash in back of me. He cleared the trail I was on—jumped right over it—and if I moved back in my tracks six feet, he would have jumped over me. He was bedded down on my left and got a whiff of me. I was between him and the top of the mountain. No sir, he wouldn't go down the mountain, or around me, he wanted to go straight up and follow that same escape route. They have habits just like we do. Even though he was that close, I just caught a glimpse of him.

I didn't have much to say to myself and I took off after him and ran myself right into the ground. He did some wicked swinging that day. He went over the mountain, then he swung down, and sloped around, and ran three or four miles straight to the top, headed northwest for a while, then swung back down the mountain. He did that four times, following the ridge, angling his swings always to the northwest, towards the high basin. I was learning to anticipate the swings and I just cut parallel to the ridge, trying to catch him when he came down. But he always was out in front of me about 200 yards and on the last swing he stayed high, and he ran hard, and he ran and ran and ran. That was the runningest deer, and it looked like a question of who in the hell was going to run out first. And it wasn't going to be me! We did about 12 miles that day, and I left him at 4:30.

Sixth Day
I went back up to the same area, just below the summit, and for the first time in the hunt I didn't find him so I

knew he was still down where I left him the day before. Rather than waste my energy going down where I know it would cost me three or four hours of tough dogging, I bypassed him and made a big swing around a swamp and looked for sign of other bucks for future hunting. I didn't find any sign of big bucks, although I saw one medium sized buck, a 4-pointer.

Seventh Day

He was back that morning, right on the very top of the mountain, hidden in the shortest spruces you could find. I got right on his trail at 7:30 but again I missed him coming out of his bed and he struck right off northwest. At around 2:00 I knew by the sign on the ground he was beginning to browse and I knew then that I might catch him so I was really pushing it when up from the valley, about 4 miles away, echoed five quick shots. It distracted me and I was looking down the side of the mountain, in open timber where you could see for up to three hundred yards. I knew my son, Lanny, was doing the shooting, for when he shoots a deer, he likes to pepper him. Just like a machine gun he is. Also, no one else was hunting this area. I never have seen another hunter or human track, we just hunt too deep in the woods for hunters to venture. Goodness, they might get lost!

So like a fool I was looking down towards the shooting, trying to imagine the scene down there. I was standing on a runway, right on the top where the big deer cross. The runway goes northwest, along the ridge and down into the big basin. But I never did catch my buck on it, because there he was, boring right at me on a collision course. I was startled at about the same time he was and when I unslung my rifle, my buck was gone and I was standing there like a fool, holding my gun.

I just wasn't thinking, and you always must keep attention in the woods. He had backtracked because the shooting startled him. He was nervous and when he saw me he reared right up, did a quick about-face, roared right back where he came from. I followed him hard until about 3:30, because I thought I'd get him but it didn't work out that way.

Eighth Day
It was a nice day for a change, not snowing and we had some sun. I picked him up at the same time in the same place and started tracking him as he moved in the same direction at the same altitude. I tracked him for 10 miles, then swung to my car. It was this day that I heard the squeal of a rabbit. I left the trail to see what was going on. A red fox had this poor old bunny rabbit and he was giving him one hell of a drubbing. He hadn't finished him when he saw me and dropped the rabbit. The rabbit is a sensitive little animal and he died right in my hands, died of fright.

Ninth Day
I found him, tracked him and didn't get a peek at him, and I was growing a little bit disgusted. I'd come home and talked about the big deer that I was following that for some reason or another kept getting away from me. I told that to Lanny and he told me, "Fine, Frank, if you can't get him, I'll have to go up and get him for you." But I didn't want him to do that. I was bothered though.

Tenth Day
All of a sudden, there he stood, in front of me, out 60 yards, and I wasn't ready for him. I had been on his track for three hours but I must have been daydream-

ing. The brush was thick and that buck backtracked like he often does. I was too nonchalant in the woods that day. Yeah, I was beginning to be careless. That day I saw where he hooked the trees, and I found where he sunk down in front of me, right before me, just looking at me. He was sneaky all right. It started to snow again and I didn't feel so sure about ever catching up with this buck.

Eleventh Day

The snow was really deep, and it was snowing a blizzard. Although I was early on his track, the snow was coming down faster than I could make out the track. So rather than spook him into an unknown country, I gave it up. I dropped down into a small plateau under the mountain and I was going through the spruces. It was quiet like in that deep snow and I came on six deer in a clearing just before a beechnut grove. I was watching them and then this buck came right up out of the snow, he just materialized, I never knew he was there, and he started browsing. These were different types of deer—mid-range deer, between the ridge runners, and the lowland deer. I was watching them and said to myself why should I shoot, I got mine to get up on the ridge, and I walked right into the midst of them. There were three buck in the group, a spikehorn, a 4 and 6-pointer. I just pointed my finger at them and went, "Bang! Bang!" They sure did take off.

Twelfth Day

It was do or die this day and I humped him for every inch of his life, boy, and I mean I petered him right out—through the spruces, hardwood, and brush. He went down to the swamp again. It had stopped snowing but it was fluffy and easy to see his tracks under the spruces, where the snow wasn't so deep. I tracked him northwest until he swung back up to where I started him. I was on his tail for about 15 miles and he followed the same routine, staying high, and I proved that he came back along the same route. That night I told my son that we'd get him the next day because I knew every move he had made was exactly the same, and we laid out our plans.

Thirteenth Day

I went up the mountain working east as I always did until I hit his track. Lanny went in east too, then swung southeast, then cut north, working slow. I jumped the buck and he rambled northwest, as I knew he would. I was still on him at about 1:00 when our mousetrap play started to work. When I was dogging him, the buck had not had human scent in front of him, but now Lanny's scent drifted up from the valley. Lanny was about 200 yards below me and the deer, working towards us.

The buck didn't know what to do so he slowed down, hesitating. I was onto his sign, right behind him, and I pussyfooted. It was a clear day, cold, but I was working a sweat. I had that feeling. The buck just couldn't figure what that was down below him. He probably never ran against two men before; this was one trick he had never had played on him, the other tricks he was wise to. I finally saw him, about 25 feet from me hidden behind a big mountain spruce, covered with snow. He was looking down the mountain in the direction of Lanny, all tense, still, suspicious looking, ears forward. I could see all his rib cage, then his shoulders and right up to his antlers. He looked bigger than ever. He was just standing there and I saw him just for a split second because my rifle was up quick. I fired, just once, and he toppled over and looked as big as a horse laying there on the ground in the deep snow. I had broken his back. I had made a poor snap shot because he was so close. He wasn't dead when I came up to him and that is when I always have my moments of regret. He and I watched each other for a few minutes and we said a few words and I said to him, "Well, we finally caught up with you didn't we?" I had to shot him again in the neck. I always hate to finish them off like that; I wish he was dead before I got there. Well, another big king went down; there're not many of the big deer left in the woods and you have to hunt a long time before you can find them. That buck had a 24-inch antler spread and dressed out at 230 pounds. I believe he would have weighed 260 pounds on that first day I spotted him.

Bucks like to leave their calling cards and so do I. I've carved my initials on beech trees in every region I've hunted—New York, Vermont, New Hampshire, Maine, Massachusetts.

The end of a successful four-day
hunt in Maine during the 1973 season.

Lanny can't help but admire the rewards of a day's hunt. He tracked this buck some 20 miles before he lined him up in his sights.

"Geez by Golly! I ain't seen nothin' like this since the 40s" said this Maine lumberman, "and they're all bucks too!" "Phtuuuey!" confirmed Uncle Windy, as he let go with a load of Red Man. "Ain't that so, feller."

My El Camino bringing in the payload in Rangeley. We caused quite a stir when we reported the deer on Main Street. "When I saw all the green shirts, I knew it had to be the Benoits," said one hunter.

When I'm in camp, I like to relax after a day's hunt with a mug of coffee and go over the day's events. I do the same thing at home during the winter months, thinking back over the many enjoyable moments I have spent in the woods during deer season.

—8—

SOUND, SIGHT, SCENT

When we go into the woods, we become hunting animals. We tune right in, and so must every hunter if he hopes to be successful. Your nose must be sharp, your ears must be extra sensitive. Everything that you hear, see, and smell should pertain to hunting. Your senses must be acute. Your body and your mind and your senses should be working together in a very tight union. When hunting you are more alert and alive than perhaps any other time in your life.

Hunting, in a way, is a very sensual sport. Without using your senses, you will not succeed. You are matching inferior senses and a superior intellect against highly tuned senses of the Whitetail whose brain is programmed to wariness and survival. It is quite a match— man against a Whitetail buck, who knows all the tricks.

SOUND

Watch a Whitetail carefully, buck or doe, when they are on the alert. Take a good look at their ears. They are just like antennas. Both ears might go straight out from the head, turned towards the front, as the deer tries to pick up a sound. Sometimes, if the sound is from the side, the deer will prick up just one ear and flop the other, trying to catch the sound. A deer might listen motionless for 15 minutes. And he can pussyfoot away quieter than you can ever hope to. Even when a deer is bedded down and asleep, its ears are constantly moving, searching for warning sounds.

The condition of the woods can affect your day's hunt. If there is high wind, I don't care to hunt. Wind makes the woods noisy and all animals become spooky when they can't hear normal woods noises. All animals just seem to disappear. Windy woods are so noisy, I become frustrated and fatigued from trying to separate the sounds I hear. I try to look extra sharp and my eyes become strained. Stay out of the woods when it is really windy and the branches are swishing and crackling and sometimes dropping and the leaves are scattering and there is a roar in the treetops. That's a good day to tell stories in deer camp, or go scouting for some new deer country.

Another time I like to stay out of the woods is when there is no snow on the ground and the leaves are frozen. The leaves become crispy as cornflakes and they make an awful racket when you walk on them. Deer far ahead can hear you, even though you are trying to be as quiet as possible.

Sometimes you will luck out. Last year Lanny shot his 10-point Maine buck when the leaves were crispy. In the morning, when he began tracking the buck, there was snow on the ground and the woods were quiet. The sun came up and on the south side of the mountain a lot of snow melted. Then the sun went under, the temperature dropped and the leaves froze. Lanny was somewhat perturbed but not about to give up. He started to walk on logs and rocks, tippy toeing, being just a hair quieter than if he walked on leaves. Even so, his walking scared up the buck he was tracking and Lanny heard him crashing through the woods. At 150 yards that buck stopped and looked back to see what had been tracking him all day. The trees lined up perfectly, leaving an open corridor between Lanny and the buck. He leaned against the tree, took two deep breaths to settle his wind and touched off his .270 the split second the red bead centered on the rib cage. The buck dropped within 50 feet. However, that was a freakish condition. Crispy leaves usually send the deer right into orbit the first time he hears you go crunch-crunch-crunch.

The best times to hunt are on still days—after or during a rain, when the woods are silent and the leaves damp and quiet as velvet—or during or just after a snowstorm. Any kind of snow (except crusty snow which is as bad as crispy leaves) is fun to hunt in, for it's quiet and all the signs are very easy to read, as easy as if it were written in a textbook.

Listen carefully in the woods. If you hear a blue jay scolding, he's giving you a tip. Something is bothering him. If I am on the trail of a buck and I hear that blue jay sound off, I pay attention, look up and around and check the woods carefully, my rifle at the ready. Many times I know how far that deer is ahead of me by the sound of these birds. Chattering squirrels also will give you warning about what's going on in the woods.

Just one crack of a branch—say a dead limb snapped off from a tree by your body, or a noise made from stepping on some dry wood—can ruin your last stalk and make you lose your buck. Last year Lanny guided Peter Miller, and twice he made noise that scared bucks. One, a 180-pounder, was scared from his bed. The other, about the same weight, was startled 40 yards

in front and crashed out of the spruces. Both noises that our friend made were slight, but these noises were enough to let that deer escape. You can see why we kiddingly call him Tanglefoot.

Walking in the woods is an art. It takes time and experience to learn. Lanny, for instance, moves very quickly when he is cruising the woods, yet he moves silently. His body sways a bit when he walks, and he uses body motion to slip between branches.

The most important part to walking is pussyfooting—when you are stalking the deer that last few hundred yards, and you know he is up there, standing about, listening, or feeding, or finding a vantage point to bed down, you cannot make any noise. Not a sound.

In this case, take your time. That buck is going nowhere unless you make a false move and warn him. Pick out your route. Glance down and figure where you are going to place your boots in the next six feet, then look up, and keep your eyes open for that buck. Don't spend all day looking at the ground. Memorize two to four steps—then look up.

If there is a tree in front of you with lots of dead branches, pick an open route around it. If there is too much brush, or a fallen tree, go around, pick the quietest route. You have time.

Do not blunder against dead limbs with your body. If necessary, use your hands to move them as you slip by. Move slowly and quietly. Harsh movements can cause that snap.

Test each step before you make it. If you bought the right boots, you can feel with your foot. Step down with your toes and instantly you can sense what's under your foot. If you feel a stick, then move the foot until you can put it down without making noise. Then put your pressure on the whole foot. If you walk in heel first, your heel will sink into the ground with more pressure than it should and do a lot more cracking of buried tree limbs.

You will find that pussyfooting is hard work. You have to keep your eyes peeled for that buck, but you also have to know where you are walking. Often this means you have to balance on one foot while you are placing the other, or do a slow motion move as you walk over a tree depression. If you lose your balance and make a sudden motion, you will scare your buck. Learn balance. Practice walking slow. Try taking short steps and lift your foot high so it doesn't drag into some obstruction that can make a noise. Place the foot under you when you take a step, and not way out in front of you. As I said, you are in no hurry. When I pussyfoot, I often sidestep when I am on a grade. I do this to keep my center of gravity right over my body so I will never be off balance. Sometimes, when I am close to a buck, I hunker down, peeking through the brush for the buck, and walk in a crouch. It can be hard work doing that, and here is another reason why you should be in good physical condition. Always remember to take a quick glance at where you are going to walk, memorize your path, then keep your eye open for buck.

If the leaves are really crispy, you must be extra careful or he'll hear you coming a mile away. You will have only one chance on your buck, for once you scare him out of his bed, or frighten him while he is feeding, he is off. Get him the first time, or forget him.

Just the jangle of coins in your pocket, the rubbing together of shells, the click of a hammer being drawn back can send your buck stampeding right out of the area.

A deer has been pawing for feed. You have to be extra quiet when you see this sign, and it's fresh.

There are times, when you are sneaking and peeking, when you don't make any noise at all, but all of a sudden you hear one awful snort just a few yards away. Shivers run up and down your back, your heart pounds and hammers, and adrenaline is just shaking you and you swing the rifle around and all you see is a white flag disappearing through the woods. You won't even have a shot. In that case, mister, that wise old Whitetail outsmarted you. That's what deer hunting is all about.

Just sling your rifle and dog his track until he slows down to a stride, then starts hooking trees or chasing does, or maybe feeding. If you've learned your lesson, you will use your eyes a lot better. It might take you half an hour or maybe two hours to catch up to that buck. You can tell what he's doing by his tracks.

SIGHT

All wild animals are well camouflaged, and that sure is true for the Whitetail buck. When the hunting season is open, the woods and ground are a bland grey-brown. So are the deer and they are very hard to spot. I know there are more times than I care to think about when that deer was peeking at me when I didn't even see him.

Your eyes should be constantly swinging and searching. You should look to the sides and dead ahead. Don't keep looking at the ground or just staring and sweeping with your eyes. You must discipline your eyes to analyze each part of the woods, trying to break down the form of a deer. It is much like working on a picture puzzle.

Every step you make is a different sight pattern and when you are sneaking up on a meandering, feeding buck, you have to look mighty careful to spot him first. When you make a step, search the woods, near and far. Bend or squat down, and do it again. Take another step, and go all over the process. You will be surprised how a deer can suddenly materialize. Just like magic.

Some hunters look for horizontal planes. They say a buck's body is horizontal, so you can spot it among the vertical trees. It's an idea to hold on to, but I find it doesn't work. It is too general. When I take the woods apart, I take it section by section, blocking it out in imaginary rectangles. I will focus close, then far, then move to the next rectangle, search it out, glance back at the first one, then move on. I am, of course, also looking for movement.

What do you see? Sometimes, when the brush is thick, all you will spot is a nose. Sometimes it is an ear and an eye. One of the bigger bucks I have shot was spotted by one eye and ear—that was all that was showing. We stared at each other for a full fifteen minutes, not moving a bit. He made the first move and my patience paid off.

During the 1966 season, Lanny was scouting for buck sign on a ridge when he heard two jays chattering and scolding. The ground was bare, and Lanny began sneaking and peeking, and tearing apart the brush with his eyes. At about 30 yards distance, through the pucker brush, he spotted a black spot which he said just didn't look like it belonged there. Lanny remained motionless and studied it some more. Finally the spot moved and antlers materialized. The black spot was the buck's nose, and the buck was curious, for it had neither heard nor seen Lanny until then. It dressed out as a 215-pound, 10-pointer.

I look for the eyes. Often their eyes are focused and gazing right down on you. A Whitetail's eyes are rimmed all around with white hair. Look for those white rims. Look for the white of the throat. Look for an ear. You might see the tail outline in white, but usually if you see the tail flicker, that buck will be gone in a split second. Never look for the flag of the tail. Some hunters do because they are bored and want to see some action and prove there is a deer there. It is then too late. A flagging tail means you've been either sloppy in your hunting or outwitted.

Remember where to look. A deer doesn't stand five foot eight; he stands about 40 inches; a big one will maybe be four feet high. When they lie down they show even less. Keep your sight patterns focused close to the ground. Watch for a tiny movement of the ears. Try to visualize your deer. If the deer is lying down, is he curled up, or is it a big buck, all stretched out? What's the outline? If he is in a bed, it will usually be above you, where he has a good sight vantage. If the deer is feeding, you'll see movement—the twitch of an ear, the switch of the tail. If he's looking at you, senses tuned, and his tail switches, then, as I said, it's another story. He's ready to motor off. Many times trophy bucks become very curious. They may backtrack and circle. So keep your eye on the track ahead, but also to the hill on the side.

Often a buck will face away from you if he feels danger, turn his head back over his shoulder and peek at you. Maybe he is standing at a slant, and his body and rack are completely hidden. He is motionless and if he gets a wrong signal, he is in the starting position for running out of there—away from you. You might be looking for a deer facing you, or standing broadside. That is the sight picture in your mind, when in reality that deer has his rump to you. His body isn't faced as you expected, except for the face looking at you—nose, eyes rimmed by white and ears. Keep your eyes peeled for these small details. Watch for antlers too, but they are difficult to spot—they look just like branches.

Often I walk out of the woods at night. Seeing your way out safely is important. I don't like to carry a flashlight because the artificial light will destroy my night vision. It takes a while for the eyes to accustom themselves to darkness. When there is snow on the ground, it is easy to see your way through the woods and I find a kind of peace when I ease my body out of the woods in the evening, walking through the snow, gazing at the first stars, and listening to the quiet of night moving in. One night I had the experience of an ermine scooting up in front of me. He pranced about like a gymnast, right at my feet. Suddenly the ermine leapt in the air, did a somersault, then scurried off. He gave me a private little show on a logging road in northern Vermont under the light of the full moon, and I thanked him for it, for treating me as a resident of the woods. He was a show-off, but he had style, the little beauty.

When it is pitch black and no snow on the ground, then you have a little difficulty. Overcast nights can cause trouble. Walk very carefully. Walk slow with your hands moving in front of your face to protect your eyes. Once you are on a log road, you will be all right, but on one of those inky black nights, darker than the center of a barrel full of molasses, you might find it better to build a fire, make a lean-to, and spend the night. That has not happened to me yet.

There's also a trick to seeing in the woods at night. Never focus directly on what you want to see. Focus above it, or to the side, and you will see what you are looking for. If you look just a little bit over the ground

you are walking on, you might spot the tree root, or tree
trunk that could trip you up.

SCENT

Many hunters and hunting books spend hours or pages
explaining the importance of scent and how to avoid having the deer smell you, and how you must hunt upwind,
crosswind, and so on. We do not pay attention to scent. I
know for a fact that in the mountains the wind will blow
four ways at once. I also know that if you get on the track
of a trophy buck, you are going to follow that track and
not stop because the wind is blowing the wrong way.

Deer will smell you. Make no doubt about it. Man
usually smells of smoke. Or bourbon. Or aftershave
scent. I can smell a man in the woods a lot faster than
I can smell a deer. If you and your clothes stink too
much, every animal on the mountainside will know
when you step from your auto and enter the woods.
Keep your smell to a minimum. Don't make it too offen-
sive for that buck. Wear clothes that are clean. Shower
before you go into the woods. The buck will smell you,
but if you are on his track he'll get used to that smell.
He'll also get curious. Lots of those poor devils were too
curious about me on their track and they met their
maker when they came back for a good look-see.

Lots of hunters swear by deer scent. I never use it. I
think the only scent attractive to a buck would be the
scent of a doe in heat. Scent made of any other thing,
such as musk glands from bucks or does I don't think
would do much except to disguise your own scent.

As I mentioned before, those farmer-hunters who
smell just like a cow seem to have pretty good luck. Lots

of people, though, don't enjoy smelling like a barnyard.

People who smoke in the woods while on the track are not using their noggins. You can spend more time fooling with your smokes instead of hunting. You should have pure mountain air in your lungs when you are on the track of a fast-moving trophy buck. Now I have a private theory about tobacco in the woods. I use Red Man chewing tobacco. There's molasses in it and I think that perhaps the bucks are attracted to that smell, at least more than they are to the scent of a sweaty, hung over, foul-breathed hunter. Stay clean in the woods, keep your scent to a minimum. Chew Red Man.

If the wind is in your favor, you can smell a buck. You can smell the difference between a cow, pig, or sheep and you can do the same in the woods with wild animals. I can smell the difference between a bear, fox, particularly a dog fox, or a hedgehog.

A buck smells of musk. It is a heavy, lingering, sweet type of smell. One morning Lanny and I were walking up a mountain. It was about 7:00 and there was fog thick as pea soup. We were joshing along, talking, just getting our second wind. I caught a whiff and told Lanny I smelled a buck. He could too. It was strong. "Let's get him!" said Lanny, and we did, within a half hour.

When you smell musk lingering in the air, you know your buck is close. Sometimes you can smell his urine if it is fresh, particularly when you are near his bed. When you catch that scent—musk or strong urine—you might, if you don't trip up somehow, be mighty close to bagging that buck.

Sound, sight, and scent. Remember these three words. If you use your senses as much as you use your brain, you should get your buck. But you must be alert, wired, and tuned into the woods and that trophy buck.

—9—
SHOOTING

A man who can't shoot straight never brings home his trophy buck, and a man with no respect for a firearm should not be allowed in the woods. I cannot say how important it is to handle a firearm safely—in your home, plinking, on a target range, walking through the woods, or shooting a deer. There are no shooting accidents—just very terrible mistakes that should never have happened.

I was brought up in a gun family. We hunted constantly, and during the Depression we counted on our guns to feed us. Yet my dad was strict about guns and I learned at a very early age his fierce concern for safety. I taught my sons respect for the firearm. If they made a mistake, even a small one—a loaded gun when it shouldn't be loaded, careless handling of it in the woods, or bantering use of it, pointing it with no thought—then they lost the right to use a gun for a year. Not only that, but I would impress on them physically their carelessness when I caught them at it. Needless to say, they know how to handle a gun safely.

I have been shot three times and each time it scared me silly. As a youngster in Vermont, I was shot in the left hip by a rimfire .32. I still don't know where the shot came from, or who shot. In New Hampshire, a small deer—we call them skippers—ran towards me and a hunter burned a four-inch groove in my leg. In both cases I was wearing red. I have since found that in many states where there is a buck and a doe season, many hunters take "sound shots." The phrase makes me quake in my boots and this is another reason I prefer to hunt where no other hunters tread.

The last time I was shot was when I was dragging out a bear in Maine. I had shot that bear under a big beech, and had carved my initials in the tree, and started to drag him down the side of a mountain. All of a sudden, a bullet hit a rock right in front of me and blew up. Shrapnel flew all over me. A small sliver struck me over the left eye and I bled like a stuck pig. I let out a holler and my hunting buddy stepped out of the trees 80 yards behind me, high on a ridge. He never saw me. I scrambled right up the bank to greet him and I muckled onto him and bounced him on the ground a bit. After that, I made him drag the bear out of the woods. That bear weighed over 300 pounds and I just marched right behind him. He broke his belt and his sling trying to drag him out but he finally made it. I'm sure he'll never forget it and I hope to God he looks carefully before he shoots. Only fools shoot at what they can't see, or don't recognize.

A lot of hunters shoot themselves. One did with his .44 magnum revolver which he had no reason to carry in the woods anyway, and no reason to shoot it. The bullet ricocheted and wounded him. Other hunters shoot themselves in the foot, leg, or body and sometimes kill themselves outright or bleed to death before they can get help. If you know your weapon, you know its safety features and you know how to carry it. If you fall down a steep bank, you should know how to handle that gun so it is not pointing at you. You always have the safety on. In the woods, the only time your finger should ever be on the trigger is when you are firing at a buck. Some people are nervous and play with the trigger and safety, testing it out. Some get tired and stagger through the woods with the rifle pointing at their foot and play with the safety. These people must be suicidal.

Always check your barrel, especially after a spill in snow. It could be plugged and burst on you when you fire. Keep your rifle in good condition. Oil the safety so it works smoothly. I always work the safety on a new gun so it smooths down then you never have to force it, or distrust it, or panic when you are trying to push the safety off and it doesn't move, or you don't think it moves and you pull the trigger by mistake.

Defensive safety is an important factor to your own well being. I never trust another hunter in the woods. When I come out of the woods onto a logging road, I always stop and get my bearings and look to see if there's anybody sitting still on the trail, especially if it's late in the afternoon. I don't want somebody to think I'm a runaway deer. I also have gotten into the habit of spotting hunters before they see me, and once I see one, I usually skirt him. If he's sitting, I give him a wide, wide berth. None of them have ever seen me, especially the stump sitters. Most of them, I believe were asleep when I went past.

Once you know the rules of safety, you have to know how to shoot. Shooting should be second nature to you. Since I was a boy, I've plinked. My spare cash went into .22 rounds and I learned to shoot cans thrown in the air, birds on the wing, and how to put bullet after bullet in the same hole—snapping the rifle to my shoulder, aiming and squeezing in one fluid motion. I practiced with revolvers, .22s, and my deer rifle. Now to keep my

It helps to practice unslinging your rifle and snapping it to your shoulder. But try it while you are moving, just as you would in the woods when a buck might surprise you.

shooting eye in trim, I use a Remington Model Nylon 66, .22 automatic carbine. I use it for partridge shooting and just plain plinking. Sometimes we set a target up about 100 yards from the house and shoot at that. Other times we tie a nail onto a string about 40 feet away and try to make the nail jump. To practice our eye on moving targets we used to put a target in an old tire and roll it down a hill while we took turns firing. My sons and I have put hours and hours in shooting and it has paid off. Shooting quickly and accurately is second nature to us, and we attribute it to years of practice.

Shooting accurately also means having a gun that fits you. Practice snapping the gun to your shoulder and pointing it instinctively at a target, without aiming. The rifle should be pointed as precisely as if you took careful aim. If your gun points low or high, work on the stock, or take it to a competent gunsmith.

Some of the best practice shooting I have had is partridge shooting with a .22. We sneak up on them and shoot them as they run through the brush, or as their bodies stop and their heads twist around. We have also shot them in flight. This is difficult shooting, for we only aim for the heads when they are on the ground. Once I had my limit this way, sitting under an apple tree as the partridge walked in during the afternoon feeding period.

We sight in our deer rifles, the 30-06 and the .270, at 50 yards. We know that the trajectory is good on the rib cage of a buck up to 200 yards. We never hold high or low when shooting our buck, but dead on. As I stated before, most of our shots are usually no more then 100 yards. Distance is not the problem, and accuracy is not the problem. A deer's rib cage averages 18 to 20 inches top to bottom and 22 to 24 inches wide. It is a mighty big target. The hardest point to shooting is when that

buck is running and there are all sorts of trees between you and the buck and a tree trunk might catch a bullet.

When we have a buck in our sights, we hold right on the rib cage, just back of the shoulder. We take no shooting positions except the ones we find we have time for, although we advocate the military rifle stances they

This drawing isn't quite accurate as there are usually many more trees blocking you from that running buck. Find an opening, hold on it, and touch your rifle off when the buck moves into the sight pattern.

used to teach with the Garand and the Springfield. We will lean up against a tree if we have time, because often we are winded from running, and can't hold the gun still. Lanny prefers to use a tree for support and cradles the gun in this arm. I like to drop to my knees and put my shoulder against a tree. We have also practiced unslinging our rifles quickly, and going into firing position and squeezing off the round in one motion. Sometimes the buck you are following might backtrack and blunder right onto you, give out an awful snort, and bolt uphill. You're so surprised that you lose your breath and your hair is standing on end, but your practice should automatically force you to bring that rifle sight into conjunction with that buck's flight.

The big problem in woods shooting is that trees do pop up between the deer and your bullet. When a deer is running, we don't lead him. We anticipate where he's running, and this is where the peep and the high front sight come in handy. We find an opening in the woods and we hold our sights onto this opening. When the deer hits the opening, and he drops into an almost folded position before his next leap, he's practically stationary and that bullet is on the way. If you shoot as you swing, chances are that you will hit a tree.

Now I often take out a little insurance by shooting several times, particularly if the brush is thick, the deer is really moving, and I never catch the deer in the folded position at the right opening. Then I hold, fire, find another opening, fire when I see hide. My last Maine buck, a 222-pound, 11-pointer, jumped out of its bed about 50 yards from me. The woods were very thick, yet I managed to put three bullets in his rib cage as he ran about 40 feet. He dropped dead within 100 feet of his bed.

By shooting the buck in the rib cage you spoil little meat, you are ensured of placing a bullet in the boiler works that will finish the deer, and the deer is quickly dead. Sometimes they will hunch up when shot. Then you know you have a true shot, and the deer will drop within yards.

For this type of shooting, I think the peepsight is the fastest. Sighting with a peepsight for me is as automatic as breathing. And with these sights you can see enough so you can track the deer while you are searching for an opening to shoot through.

You know, a fellow can throw a tin can up in the air and pick it off with some kind of gun but shooting at a trophy buck which is a million times bigger than a can, well, the problem is, lots of people get excited. They get buck fever. You can't get excited, you have to stay calm and cool. If you shoot enough, and concentrate on hitting that buck, you can't get buck fever. Yet, I've pointed out bucks to friends in the woods and they just stared

and forgot to shoot. One got to gatling, emptied his gun at the buck, missing it by a mile while that stunned buck just stood there. He reloaded and shot again and emptied his rifle. I got to laughing so hard that the buck finally took off. Buck fever saved that buck's skin.

It is damned rare when we wound a deer but it has happened. Most hunters will tell you to sit down, cool off, have a cigarette, and wait until the deer stiffens up. Then go after him. I don't believe in that at all. By waiting and fooling around you give the deer mending time. The blood coagulates and plugs the hole up. A deer sure won't stiffen up in 20 minutes. If you have put a bullet into a deer, and he's bleeding heavily, push 'im. Pretty soon, the blood will be all out of him. I've seen wounded deer get out of their bed with a bullet in their leg as fast as if they didn't even have a bullet in them.

Once you have downed your buck, approach him warily, usually from the head. He might be wounded, stunned, or dead, but if he is wounded or stunned he might bound up, feet flashing and you could be seriously hurt. Touch his eyes with the end of your gun barrel. If they blink, he is alive. Sometimes you have to finish off your buck with a shot. I am always sorry to see one of those trophy bucks lying at the end of the trail, yet his being there is a sign of a successful hunt. I make my peace with him, and if necessary, shoot him in the neck. I never, never shoot a buck in the head. They are too glorious an animal for that type of treatment.

I am sorry about many of the tragic sights I have seen in the woods. I have seen does wounded by irresponsible hunters. I have seen fawns with gaping wounds in their legs. I have seen young spikehorn bucks and does and fawns lying dead from being carelessly and needlessly shot. I feel ashamed for the actions of some so-called hunters. All a hunter has to do is to take a few seconds to look over what he's going to shoot. Unfortunately, I think too many hunters kill for the sake of killing. That is not hunting. That is mayhem. People like this should take up karate, or go bar brawling. There is no reason in the world to shoot wildly, without thought, and cause torture to such a magnificent game animal. My sons' and my purpose is to hunt for the trophy buck and not for the killing. We always regret knocking down those big bucks. But we are proud that we had the skill to outwit him, and kill cleanly.

–10–
DRESSING AND DRAGGING OUT YOUR BUCK

You thought you worked hard trying to get your trophy buck. Now that you've got him, lying right there before you deep in the woods, and you've made your peace with this majestic animal, now, friend, your work has only begun.

Dressing out your buck seems to be just a mean, ornery job, but it is one of the most important jobs to do correctly. If you make a mistake in dressing out the buck, you can kiss good-bye some of the choice pieces of meat. Dress your buck out as soon as possible. Don't leave that buck. Don't go for help. Don't do anything until he is dressed properly. An undressed buck left a few hours with the guts in could ruin it, and leaving it overnight is disastrous. The natural gases that form in the stomach and intestines seem to back up through the entire bloodstream and leave the meat with an odor and taste that is not pleasant. You can smell it before it's cooked and after it's cooked. Some people it doesn't bother, but me, I wouldn't eat one.

A lot of people stick their deer by cutting the neck. For what reason? The animal is already dead. I never heard of anyone sticking a dead hog. You have already shot the deer. You're going to open the deer up and you're going to start from the windpipe and go all the way to the rear. So when you take out the lung, heart, liver, intestines, and stomach, doesn't that make sense that you are cutting all arteries that lead to the main supply—the heart? So if the heart is removed from the body, what's the sense in cutting its throat?

A lot of people castrate their bucks. Why? It's a tradition and I know the Indians cut off the testicles—Rocky Mountain Oysters—and ate them. They were good to eat and besides some believed they were rejuvenative. But the Indians never threw anything away, and the first thing they ate off their deer were the oysters, the heart, and the liver. The Plains Indians even cleaned the intestines to store pemmican—fats and fruits and nuts mixed together. It was seasoned something like our sausage. The Plains Indians wouldn't waste anything from their deer, just as the Eastern Indians didn't.

I must admit I never ate mountain oysters. But I would if we were over in camp and decided to try them. I cut off the testicles because it is a tradition. It is one of the signs of a successful hunt. When I was a child I would cut off the testicles and take them home to show them to my family, because often they wouldn't believe I shot a big buck. It is living proof that the animal is dead and I have yet to hear of a deer running around the mountain with his nuts cut off.

The first thing I do before I even take my knife out is to roll the deer on his back. If there is a depression in the area, try to get the center of the buck in that depression. It helps to hold him. Grab one of his legs and push it upright until his back is laying on the ground. The leg will be in the air. Hold it there by straddling the deer and keep the buck's leg in the air by using your leg as a brace.

To castrate the buck, make a slit in the bag, then squeeze at the base of it and the testicles will pop out. In that way you'll only have an inch slit in the bag and there's no big mess. Some hunters cut off the whole bag and you end up with a big bloody area exposed to flies and dirt.

There has been a lot of controversy on removing the musk glands on the hocks of the back leg. Some people swear they will ruin the meat, others don't. I don't take them off and my deer meat has usually been very sweet. Here just use your own discretion. If you want to take them off, then put the knife right to them.

Now starts the slitting of the deer. While straddling the deer, facing the head, find where the soft stomach muscles end and the chest bones begin. Take the very tip of your knife with the butt of the knife pointed at the deer's throat or at an approximate 45° angle. Use just the tip of your knife to go through the hide.

Cut a couple of inches towards you until you have an opening big enough to see what you are doing. Once

the hide is cut, the cutting will be easy. Once you cut through the stomach muscles, you can insert two fingers and place the blade between your fingers. The fingers act as a guide for the knife blade. (But be careful! Go slow.) The reason that the buck is on his back is to keep the intestines away from the incision. You don't want to cut those intestines and you don't want those juices on the meat, for they can penetrate that meat just like gasoline. Cut about a 12 to 16-inch gash in his belly muscles, back to the pelvic area.

Now cut a small stick about 10 inches or longer, depending upon how big the buck is. Some trophy bucks will need a stick 14 to 16 inches long. Take the stick and put it into the incision and spread open the stomach flanks so everything is exposed.

Cut the diaphragm—the muscle that separates the intestines from the heart and lungs. Reach in, holding the blade of your knife with your thumb and forefinger, allowing only a quarter-inch of knife cutting edge showing, and cut the diaphragm from the backbone to the rib cage. You must cut the diaphragm on the right and left side of the rib cage to free heart and lungs and liver from the intestines.

Then reach into the chest cavity, beyond the lungs as far as you can reach into the brisket, and then cut the windpipe. Pull the heart, lungs, and liver gently through the diaphragm which you have already cut.

As you pull out the heart, lungs, and liver, some membranes will be holding the organs to the backbone. Have your knife close to the backbone and cut those membranes away, being careful not to cut the intestines. By being careful in the beginning, and not being squeamish, you'll do a good job. The heart, lungs, liver, intestines, and stomach paunch will all roll out. If the stick is in the way so the innards can't flop out, move it, but keep the stomach cavity open so you can see what you are doing.

After the viscera is rolled out of the cavity, one of the most crucial operations is the urine bladder. You must be very careful. If that bladder is full, reach up to the pelvic bone and grasp the bladder by the ureter, the tube that leads to it, and twist it and pinch it as tight as you can. Then snip it off with your knife blade, being extra careful not to relax your grip. Take it out and get it away from the meat. One drop of buck urine inside the body cavity and it spreads just as quickly as stomach gases.

Now reach back in and grab hold of the big intestine and pull it towards you. This brings all the deer turd back into the intestine. Now snip it off. Wipe your hands off in the leaves or in the snow so you don't get blood all over yourself or the antlers of your trophy buck. Move your trophy to a clean area, or to a brook if there's one nearby. Roll your buck on his belly, spread all four legs, pointing the chest cavity uphill with the stick in the stomach cavity, keeping it open. Let him drain clean for about five minutes, while you clean yourself and your equipment. Sit down and relax. Have a smoke, if you smoke, or have a chew. If you prefer the heart and liver, put it in that plastic bag you've been carrying. Take what you want. Go back to your trophy after he is drained out and look in to see if anything else is left in there you want to take out. Be sure all the blood is out. If you want to clean him out, there are thousands of little paper towels lying all around you—leaves. Take the cleanest layer of top leaves and use them as a rag to sponge up the inside of the deer until everything is dry. You can also use snow.

Take the stick out of the cavity and the incision will close up. In two or three hours, that incision will close up firmly. If you have a long drag, the small incision will keep leaves and dirt from getting into it. On snow you have no problem.

Take that nice piece of five-foot quarter-inch nylon rope that has been hanging off your gun belt. Make a loop and put it around the base of the horns. Make a half hitch and put it around his nose. Take your knife and find a nice little sapling about an inch and a half through. Cut a piece 24 to 30 inches long, depending upon how long you like it. Bring it back and tie that rope to the stick. Make a double check around the area to see you haven't left your favorite knife, rifle, lunch, or knapsack before you take off. If you leave anything, leave your initials on a tree.

Point your nose towards your car and pull. And pull. If it is on snow, he will weigh less than what you think he does. But if he is on bare ground, he's going to weigh a lot more than you think he weighs.

Stay high until you have an idea where your car is, then swing down. If you have a long road to follow, you're lucky. Otherwise, head down but stay out of ravines, and don't head towards roaring brooks, which means banks, boulders and all sorts of hauling trouble with a big buck.

A high mountain doesn't necessarily mean a tough drag. I have dragged a 235-pound deer two miles in three hours, but it was all a downhill drag on snow. If you come off snow and onto bare ground, it may take you half a night to reach your car that is only a half mile away. If you have friends you're hunting with, maybe you should arrange a signal. I usually don't have people help me during hunting hours because I figure I shouldn't ruin a day's hunting for them.

The longest drag I ever had was two days. It was a 235-pound 8-pointer. It was a good six-mile haul. I dragged all afternoon and half a night, then left it, and came back the next day, with four of my family. It took us all day, on bare ground, for two or three miles.

Rest while you're dragging. Don't overexert yourself. If you're hungry make a hot fire out of dry dead wood.

Reach in and take a piece of tenderloin out of the body cavity next to the backbone. If you're near a stream, wash it off, otherwise—just eat it like my Indian ancestors used to. I put the meat on a stick and broil it over the coals. After it is seared, I add the salt and pepper and bacon grease, which I carry mixed together in a plastic bag. There's no finer meal you'll ever have, particularly if it is at night, and the stars are bright, and you're gaunter than a frog and twice as hoppy. It will be a meal you'll never forget, and it will give you the energy to drag that buck to your car.

I repeat—the main thing is not to overexert yourself, particularly hunters with a heart condition. Leave your buck and blaze a trail and come back with your buddies. Don't get overly excited. When you're tired, sit down and admire your trophy until your excitement wears off. Take it easy.

Warning—this is essential. In some states, you are not allowed to drag that buck one inch until the tag is tied onto the antlers or in his ear. One false move on your part in violation of the law could cost you your trophy which you worked so hard to get.

Sometimes people who I won't even call hunters will be so abominable as to steal your buck. I have my rifle, and no one ever took a deer away from me.

Once I was dragging out a buck and as I came to a log road I could smell cigarette smoke coming on the wind from below me so I hid the deer and came to a pickup with four hunters who were kind of shaggily dressed. They had been drinking. One of them asked if I had shot up on the ridge.

"Might have been." I said.

"What'd you shoot, a doe?" he asked.

"No, I didn't shoot any doe!" I snapped back.

"Who are you?" he said. "I'm the deputy game warden."

"Let me see your credentials."

"I don't have to show them to you. What'd you shoot?"

"It's none of your damn business."

"You're talking kind of tough. There's four of us." "Yeah," I replied, "and there's six of us," and I patted my rifle.

They skedaddled down the road but before they left they said they were going to backtrack me in the morning and see what I got.

"Have fun," I said. I went down the main road, picked up my son, drove back up, and hauled out that 9-point buck.

If you do have to leave a buck in the woods, and are afraid someone will take your buck, cut a slash in the buck's knee joint that separates the outer skin from the inner skin, and insert a coin in it and memorize the date and denomination of the coin. That is absolute positive identification, and you can identify that stolen deer right there in front of the hunter and the game warden. After proving it, beat the living daylights out of the dirty thief.

−11−

HANGING, BUTCHERING, AND COOKING

What makes a deer good eating? There are lots of reasons. Much of it depends upon what the deer has been eating. A deer feeding on buds, nuts, mushrooms, and fiddlehead ferns is usually awfully good eating. Some I have shot were so tough you couldn't cut the gravy. I don't know just what causes that but sometimes it is hemlock, which deer will eat even when there's good food right in front of them. It acts like a laxative on them.

I do know this. The little cusses aren't always the tender ones. My son Lance once shot a 115-pound spikehorn. We were really anxious to cut into that one, for we thought we were going to have some good eating. But it was tough and awful. Young bucks run a lot. The trophy buck doesn't run as much. He moves but he's not running except when he has you or me on his tail. The big buck is awfully good eating. So is an old one, one of those rangy critters that lives on wild browse on the top of mountains and has never been bothered by humans or dogs.

If you have dressed your buck properly the next item, when you have it home, is to hang it properly. In Vermont, I let my deer hang sometimes for a month. I let the meat cure. Hanging tenderizes the venison. Sometimes I let them hang so long some neighbors think

I'm just showing off my bucks. One said that he knew that after they hung so long, I just threw them in the dump. A woman called me up and told me I might as well give her the meat instead of throwing it away. I have never thrown a deer away, and there's little waste after I butcher it. Maybe the next time I should bring that woman the box of waste I have after I butchered a deer.

When you hang a buck, always hang it by its hindquarters. A buck is too magnificent an animal to be hung by its head. I hang him from my porch, or the tree in the front yard. If it's cold out, I'll hang him for a month. Otherwise, I'll hang him for a week or 10 days.

The first thing to do is spread the rib cage with another stick and clean out the blood, dirt, and leaves with a rag soaked in vinegar, or with salt. Then I wipe the cavity dry.

Then, boil water and salt until an egg can float in it. Take a paintbrush and paint the inside of the body cavity with salt water. One coat should do it. I plug the bullet holes inside and out with raw salt. I just pour it right in. That's it. Then just leave the buck to cure. Blowflies will not attack your buck. I guarantee it.

If the deer is badly shot up in the shoulder, pelvic, neck, or back area, or whenever big bones are broken, do not wait too long a period before cutting up. Then I would let it hang no more than three or four days. This is another good reason to keep your shots in the rib cage. You don't ruin much meat by shooting into the ribs. You can ruin a whole shoulder by smashing into a shoulder joint.

Lots of hunters don't have the space or the right climate to hang their own buck. Take it to a butcher and have him hang it for you.

Now for your trophy head, which will be a source of

We butcher our venison right in our own home.

pride for years and years. Many conversations will come up with your friends after gazing at the rack in your den. I always take mine to a good taxidermist. If you are keeping the head for a week or 10 days, separate the skin from the head. Cut a straight line from the back of the head to between the two horn bases. Skin out the entire head being very careful to do a good job. After the head is separated from the skull, spread out the cape and salt it very well. Roll it up and keep it in a cool place. If you want to cut the antlers off, go ahead. Take a meat saw and lop off the top section of the skull with the antler and your taxidermist will smooth it out the way he wants to. I suggest you check with your taxidermist for details on how he prefers it.

The easiest method, though, is to cut off the head at the neck and let the taxidermist take it off where he wants it. You might want to save the hooves for a gun rack. Cut them off at the hock and send them to the taxidermist with the cape and horns, or the whole head.

A butcher will do all the skinning for you but if you intend to cut up your own deer, you start by skinning him when he is hanging. All I can say is skin very carefully, using a skinning knife that is as sharp as you can get it. Slit from the middle of the deer's crotch to the gambrel on both rear legs. Let the hide fold back from the meat as you work it off. Pull, then cut a bit, being very careful not to cut into the hide. Take your time. And remember to keep dirt off the meat.

After you have removed the hide, scrape off any meat or fat that clings to it. I use an old file with handles on both ends. Then salt it down, roll it up, and leave it in a cool place until you are ready to have it tanned.

If you wish to do your own tanning, you can buy a professional tanning kit. Or you can do it the old Indian way, the method I used as a child when I made shirts and pouches. Take a solution of tallow (rancid fats) and mix it with hardwood ashes, then rub it into the hide, work it with your hands until it is deep into the hide. To take the hair off, soak the hide for eight to 10 days in a mild solution of water and ashes. Take it out, pull the hair out, then rinse it out. If you find the hide is still tough, smoke it over hardwood chips. But let me tell you, unless you have time on your hands, send it to your taxidermist, or to a shop that specializes in tanning or in making buckskin clothes.

Only do your own butchering if you know what you are doing. It is extremely easy to ruin a lot of good meat by cutting against the grain or across the grain, or hacking away at what you think is a joint, until you find you've missed it altogether.

You need a good place to do your butchering. I use the dining room table, but most of you have wives who would scream bloody murder, and justifiably, I guess. So find a good worktable in someplace that will placate your wife. You need a meat saw, boning knives, and steak slicing knives. Steaks you cut from the haunch. Chops come from the backbones. You can end up with back roasts, if you don't want chops. Other choice pieces are the rump roasts. The neck is good for pot roast, the front shoulders for soups and stews. Deerburgers can also come from the neck or rib cage. As venison has little fat in it, I mix in beef suet with the deerburgers. I also crack the bones to make soup. When our children were small we always had a pot full of venison bone soup for them when they came home from school.

Butchering is a personal choice and there are many ways to do it. I, for instance, like my steaks and chops cut to ¾ inch. You might light them thicker or thinner.

If you have any doubt about this whole process, take your buck to a butcher and tell him what you want as to steaks, chops, roasts, stew meat, and deerburger.

As fast as I cut my deer, my wife Iris wraps it and puts in in our freezer. I have little wasted meat because I place my shots in the rib cage, so we usually end up with enough venison to last through the year and give some away to friends.

Now the real joys during the months after your hunt are in preparing and eating your venison. My wife Iris has been cooking venison for 34 years and included here are some of her recipes, plus a few others she has made up for supplying us with food while we are in camp or on the track.

POT ROAST OF VENISON

I use the shoulder. If it is a big buck, I cut it in two and just use one half. Put it in a heavy pot with a chunk of beef fat, about ⅛th of a pound. It keeps the venison moist and adds flavor. Beef fat can be bought in most supermarkets. Let the meat brown in the pot, turning it now and then. Add water. As it boils down, add more until the meat is tender. Add three bouillon cubes, three whole onions, ⅛th teaspoon of garlic powder, salt and pepper to taste, and one tablespoon of Worcestershire sauce.

New add six peeled carrots and six peeled potatoes. Let cook until tender.

Make a flour and water paste and stir until smooth. I use ½ cup of flour, ½ cup of water. Put this to one side. If you want, add ½ cup mushrooms to the stock. Let cook about five minutes. Take the meat out, stir the flour and water paste into the stock to make a gravy and serve.

VENISON STEW

Cut up into small pieces 1½ pounds of venison about one inch by one inch. This can be pieces from the lower part of the leg or parts cut off from the steak. Put into a heavy pot with pieces of beef fat. Let this brown, stirring the pieces of meat. After it browns, keep adding a little water and let it cook down. Watch it closely so it doesn't burn. Do this until the meat is tender. Now add three bouillon cubes, one tablespoon of Worcestershire sauce, and salt and pepper to taste. Add two whole onions, and ⅛ teaspoon of garlic powder.

Cut up four carrots and four potatoes, add and cook until tender. Add one small can of mushrooms or fresh mushrooms if you have them.

Mix three tablespoons of flour and ½ cup of water until smooth. Stir this into the stew until it thickens. Turn down the heat from medium to low.

For dumplings, mix three cups of flour, three teaspoons of baking powder, one teaspoon of salt, ½ cup of shortening, and add one cup of milk. Drop by the spoonful into the stew and put cover on. Let cook 10 minutes at medium heat.

DEER HEART

Wash the heart well. Boil the heart with beef fat, salt, and pepper until tender. Slice the heart crosswise, then sauté with one teaspoon Worcestershire sauce, three slices onions, some beef fat, and add a little garlic powder.

STEAK AND CHOPS

Do just like regular steaks. Get the pan good and hot and add beef fat. Sear the steaks on both sides to keep in the juices. We generally serve our venison steaks and chops medium rare.

BROWNIES

This gives lots of energy while you are in the woods. Melt in a double boiler sauce pan 4 squares of chocolate and ½ pound of butter. Then add two cups of sugar, one teaspoon of vanilla and stir. Now add four eggs and stir. When smooth, add 2¾ cups of flour and stir in. Add one teaspoon of baking powder, ½ cup of walnuts. Cook at 350 F. for 30 minutes. I use a Pyrex cake pan.

BANNOCK

This is good in the camp and can be carried dry in a plastic bag. Mix one cup of flour and one teaspoon of baking soda and ½ teaspoon of salt. Just add water until it is doughy. Cook on frying pan or over a hot rock. It is especially good when served with maple syrup that has been boiled down to an extra thick consistency.

-12-

THOUGHTS ON HUNTING

There are many times that I've sat down and wondered just what hunting means to me—why it is such an important part of my life. Hunting has been a tradition in our family, yet some members have inherited more of the hunting instinct than others. I cannot explain why, but the hunting urge ran deep in my father. It courses through my veins, and lives within my sons.

Man began as a hunter, and lived by his senses until reason made him the most destructive of all animals. Yet through the ages of so called civilization, man has retained the sport of hunting as one of his primary avocations. The spirit of hunting has been traced to the Iron Age.

To me, tracking a buck is happiness. We have little enough time to enjoy ourselves in this life. We must work hard to exist, and we do many things we don't like to do. Hunting is a happy occupation, and I consider it not only a privilege, but a right, particularly in my home, the glorious state of Vermont. Our mountains have traditionally been open to hunters, although now many out-of-state landowners who never walk their boundaries are selfishly posting it.

Come November and the opening of buck season and I have my annual catharsis. I'm renewed with the enthusiasm of burying myself deep in the wilderness, tracking down that wily buck. I feel in my bones the traditions of our hunting past. I feel alive when I move along a mountainside. Life quickens for me. My pulse bounds. There is mystery and electricity and magic in the air—it throbs through my whole body. There is lingering in me that anticipation of fulfillment that is also felt when it's time to make love.

Hunting, or the chase, is outwitting the animal. And the culmination of the hunt is death. This ritual brings me home to existence. I become part of what has made me—the sun, earth, the seasons, death and life. I feel this keenly in the woods—living, existing, and also dying. It is a humbling, almost religious experience. I do not take joy in killing. There is little thrill in that. Everyone of us has those moments of regret after we've knocked down one of those big bucks. To me, the thrill is being able to trail a trophy buck and get him in my sight, knowing I could kill him anytime I wanted to.

I like to kill cleanly and quickly. I don't want such a magnificent animal as the Whitetail to suffer. Yet I am proud of my achievement in being able to outwit a large, smart trophy buck. I also take great enjoyment in supplying meat to my family. Sweet venison is a delicacy I will always enjoy.

There are other factors I love about hunting—I like the freshness of the woods, for there I can find peace and order. There are no social restrictions that inhibit my mind when I cruise the woods. There is no traffic, no smells, no signs ordering me about. There is nothing but the natural laws of the wilderness which I feel at home with.

I love the beauty of the woods. Once you become a hunter and catch the electricity of the hunt, you become a part of the woods, you melt right into the surroundings

as another member of the wild. There is an inward beauty in this, just as there is an outward beauty in a rushing, splashing mountain stream, or in a patch of moss, deep green, that surrounds some hidden spring where the deer come to sip, or the symmetry of a smooth barked beech tree, scarred by old bear claw marks. I admire the wild beauty I discover when standing on mountaintops, looking into hidden basins and bowls, and seeing no sign of civilization—neither houses, roads, nor other hunters. I find magic in the way the sun lights the woods in the early morning and late afternoon. I feel repose in a wilderness snowstorm when the flakes drift down as delicately as thistledown and the ground becomes as soft as white velvet and the snow frosts the spruces and there is no wind—only silence. I savor the wind that bites and whips my face on the summit of a mountain, searing the flesh as it slashes down from the northwest. I like to feel my heart thump as I trot after a buck, and I move up and down mountainsides, and catch my second breath and know that I am in tune with that animal I'm tracking.

I love the smell of clean mountain air, and the taste of water that bubbles down the draws—clear, cold, sweet. I enjoy meeting my woods friends—the chickadees, those curious little birds, that will hop on my hand and share my sandwich, the chipmunks and red squirrels that flirt with me, more curious than a buck ever hopes to be.

Then, of course, there is nothing more beautiful to watch than the Whitetail, graceful in all movements. Even when they bound away from me, I can't help but admire their fluid beauty. And I admire their wily spirit, their wariness, for it is these qualities that make them such a sought after trophy. You cannot buy this trophy.

One must imitate the deer to be a successful hunter—learn his habits and act as he does. It is this quality that appeals to me so much. I become what I feel in my bones—the instinctive hunter. I have more of a yearning to live and act and relate to the wild environment and laws of nature—not to civilization, which can clutter and rot our brains and senses.

L.E.B.

Bagging a trophy buck is an experience that you will always fondle in your memories.

LARRY BENOIT'S SCORECARD

Whitetail Bucks Shot in Vermont

Year	Age of Larry	Weight of Deer	No. of Points
1933	9	over 200	8
1934	10	over 185	7
1935	11	over 175	6
1936	12	over 205	8
1937	13	over 208	6
1938	14	over 195	5
1939	15	No deer	
1940	16	over 210	8
1941	17	over 175	6
1942	18	over 145	6
1943	19	No deer	
1944	20	185	8
1945	21	195	8
1946	22	185	8
1947	23	195	8
1948	24	207	7
1949	25	212	8
1950	26	210	7
1951	27	215	8
1952	28	225	9
1953	29	135	4
1954	30	135	6
1955	31	212	7
1956	32	210	7
1957	33	185	8
1958	34	215	10
1959	35	135	7
1960	36	230	8
1961	37	175	4
1962	38	185	7

An 11-point, 222-pounder I took in Maine. The base of the antlers is 5⅝ inches

Year	Age of Larry	Weight of Deer	No. of Points
1963	39	195	8
1964	40	134	4
1965	41	145	5
1966	42	235	8
1967	43	225	10
1968	44	215	8
1969	45	160	6
1970	46	230	8
1971	47	202	9
1972	48	215	13
1973	49	210	10

Whitetail Bucks Shot in Maine

Year	Age of Larry	Weight of Deer	No. of Points
1972	48	215	13
1973	49	222	11

Totals

Number of Years Hunted 41
Number of Deer 41
Average Weight 193.8
Average Number of Points 7.6

My son, Lanny, with a 10-point, 242-pound Maine buck.

LANNY BENOIT'S SCORECARD

Whitetail Bucks Shot in Vermont

Year	Age of Lanny	Weight of Deer	No. of Points
1955	9	165	4
1956	10	160	2
1957	11	175	7
1958	12	163	6
1959	13	175	5
1960	14	175	7
1961	15	200	9
1962	16	165	6
1963	17	200	11
1964	18	145	2
1965	19	205	9
1966	20	215	10
1967	21	175	9
1968	22	230	7
1969	23	235	10
1970	24	230	8
1971	25	244	8
1972	26	220	10
1973	27	235	10

Whitetail Bucks Shot in Maine

Year	Age of Lanny	Weight of Deer	No. of Points
1972	26	215	9
1973	27	242	10

Totals

Number of Years Hunted 19
Number of Deer 21
Average Weight 198.5
Average Number of Points. 7.5